Cambridge Computer Science Texts · 10

Computers and Social Change

Murray Laver

CAMBRIDGE UNIVERSITY PRESS

CAMBRIDGE

LONDON   NEW YORK   NEW ROCHELLE

MELBOURNE   SYDNEY

Published by the Press Syndicate of the University of Cambridge

The Pitt Building, Trumpington Street, Cambridge CB2 1RP

32 East 57th Street, New York, NY 10022, USA

296 Beaconsfield Parade, Middle Park, Melbourne 3206, Australia

First published 1980

Printed in the United States of America

Library of Congress Cataloguing in Publication Data

Laver, F.J.M.
    Computers and social change

    (Cambridge computer science texts ; 10)
    Includes bibliographies and index.
    1. Computers and civilization.   2. Social change.
I. Title.   II. Series.
QA76.9.C66L38   001.6'4   79-19329
ISBN 0 521 23027 6   hard covers
ISBN 0 521 29771 0   paperback

Contents

		Page
Preface		vii
Chapter 1	MEN, WOMEN AND COMPUTERS	
1.1	Prudence or timidity?	1
1.2	Computer characteristics	2
1.3	Prediction	5
1.4	The assessment of technology	6
1.5	Computers and society	9
1.6	Bibliography	10
	Examples 1	11
Chapter 2	INFORMATION AND SOCIETY	
2.1	Information systems	12
2.2	Viewdata	14
2.3	Some matters of policy	15
2.4	The rich and the poor in information	18
2.5	Bibliography	20
	Examples 2	21
Chapter 3	SOME ECONOMIC EFFECTS	
3.1	Introduction	23
3.2	Economics and its data	23
3.3	The use of numerical data	24
3.4	Precision, accuracy and significance	26
3.5	Computers and economic analysis	28
3.6	Computers and common sense	31
3.7	Bibliography	31
	Examples 3	32

Chapter 4   COMPUTERS AND EMPLOYMENT

    4.1   Computers and productivity   34

    4.2   Productivity and employment   35

    4.3   Microcomputers, automation and employment   38

    4.4   Employment and social change   40

    4.5   System design for service, or efficiency?   42

    4.6   Work sharing   44

    4.7   Bibliography   45

         Examples 4   46

Chapter 5   EDUCATION AND LEISURE

    5.1   Introduction   47

    5.2   Education, work and computers   47

    5.3   The problem of leisure   49

    5.4   Computer-assisted instruction   52

    5.5   Computer arts and crafts   54

    5.6   Games and other amusements   55

    5.7   Coda   56

    5.8   Bibliography   57

         Examples 5   58

Chapter 6   THE DOMESTICATED COMPUTER

    6.1   Introduction   59

    6.2   Some household systems   60

    6.3   Domestic appliances   62

    6.4   Miscellaneous services   63

    6.5   Telecommunications   64

    6.6   Some social consequences   67

    6.7   Bibliography   68

         Examples 6   69

Chapter 7   PRIVACY AND THE PROTECTION OF DATA

    7.1   Introduction   70

    7.2   Privacy defined   70

7.3	Personal data files	71
7.4	The users of personal data	74
7.5	Computers and personal data	76
7.6	Some principles	77
7.7	Data protection and the law	78
7.8	Coda	79
7.9	Bibliography	80
	Examples 7	81

Chapter 8	CRIME AND WAR	
8.1	Computers and crime	83
8.2	Police and security	86
8.3	Computer system security	89
8.4	Computers and war	92
8.5	Bibliography	94
	Examples 8	95

Chapter 9	SYSTEMS AND SOCIETY	
9.1	System integrity	96
9.2	A highly strung society	99
9.3	The systems concept	101
9.4	Coda	103
9.5	Bibliography	104
	Examples 9	104

Chapter 10	COMPUTERS AND DEMOCRACY	
10.1	Introduction	106
10.2	The will of the people	106
10.3	Computer modelling and political choice	109
10.4	Computers and corporativism	110
10.5	Coda	111
10.6	Bibliography	112
	Examples 10	113

Chapter 11   THE WAY AHEAD

    11.1   Side-effects and society   114

    11.2   The case for social control   114

    11.3   Methods of social control   115

    11.4   Choosing our future   118

    11.5   Coda   119

Index   121

Preface

In recent years there has been a growing realization that computers are very much more than fast automatic calculating machines for accountants and scientists; and a deepening concern has arisen about the possible consequences of their widespread use. This concern has been sharpened by the advent of the microcomputer. Some of the consequences raise problems that involve economic, social and political considerations which lie beyond the specific expertise of computer specialists. It is important, therefore, to promote the closest cooperation and understanding between all who are engaged in designing or using computer systems, or who may be affected by their operation.

This book is intended to contribute to the improvement of understanding by delineating the principal problem areas. Its subject falls into one of those awkward interdisciplinary gaps, but an attempt has been made to present it in such a way that it will be useful not only for making computer specialists aware of the external implications of their work, but also for informing non-specialists about the ways in which the application of computers may affect the lives of every one of us.

The treatment seeks to follow a realistic middle way, avoiding both the doom-ridden pessimism that predicts a future inevitably dominated by machines, and the facile optimism of the more naive technocratic utopias. The content is based on a short course which has been given at the University of Newcastle-upon-Tyne, and on occasional lectures elsewhere, and the author is grateful to all who have listened patiently, and especially to those who have interrupted constructively during the last four years.

Sidmouth, Devon
1979   F.J.M.L.

1 · Men, women and computers

1.1 Prudence or timidity?

The consequences of adopting a new technology have often
exceeded our expectations as its effects spread well beyond the
original application to influence men, women and society in ways
that were not foreseen by the innovators; and which soon passed
beyond their power to control, even had they wished to do so.
Thus the internal combustion engine began simply enough as an
improved type of power plant, but by fostering the rapid growth
of air and road transport it has vastly increased our mobility,
created new industries, and left us with some very difficult
social and economic problems. Technologists commonly claim
that their art is neutral, but they can offer no guarantee that
everyone will use it for the benefit of mankind, nor that it is
free from troublesome side-effects. Some of the uses of technology in peace and in war have made us wary and, in common
with nuclear energy and genetic engineering, computers are seen
by many as a part of that application of science to advanced
industrialization which threatens to make our lives unpleasant,
empty or brief.

A century ago an *entrepreneur* was not at all concerned with
such incidental effects of his activity as pollution or redundancy; they were not likely to affect him personally, and public
opinion did not censure him for overlooking what might happen to
his workers or their environment. On the contrary, he expected
to be praised for creating wealth and providing employment.
Things are different today: indeed, we could be in danger of
swinging to the opposite extreme and losing benefits because we
are often more ready to see problems than to seize opportunities.

The line between prudence and timidity is a narrow one, but

l to draw it carefully if we are to act wisely and yet
falling into a dreary neurosis. Our task is not made
by the media of mass information which, often acting as
if good news were no news, emphasize the hazards, the problems
and the conflicts, and only rarely proclaim the successes or
expound the benefits of technical advance. Certainly they perform a useful public service by drawing attention to unpleasant
social consequences, for these are apt to escape mention by
those who are promoting a new project. But they also leave the
impression that adverse consequences abound and are inescapable,
and that the balance of advantage is weighted against society,
whereas none of these is universally true.

1.2 Computer characteristics

The public's distrust of technology in general is not
sufficient to explain the widely expressed worries about the
effects of computers on society. There are additional reasons
which derive from the specific characteristics of computer
systems.

First, it is now generally realized that computers are
much more than mere calculating machines, however fast or
automatic. A computer is controlled by a program of instructions which we have written to guide it step-by-step through a
sequence of operations that will perform some work we wish it
to do. When necessary, this sequence can be long, intricate
and adaptive, and the work correspondingly complex. More im-
portantly, a computer's current program can readily be replaced
by another, which enables us to set it up quickly and easily
for any of a large number of tasks. Indeed, it can perform
several different tasks concurrently by switching automatically
from one program to another and back again in a small fraction
of a second.

Next, computers are not limited to arithmetic. They can
handle any kind of data that we know how to represent by

2

symbols: numerals, letters, punctuation marks, conventional signs or diagrams, for instance. Very large amounts of data can be taken in, stored, and rapidly recalled when we are ready to deal with them, which we can then do in whatever way we know how to specify (and thus to program). The processes we apply to our data may include arithmetical, logical, probabilistic, arbitrary or even random operations. Obviously it must be possible to complete them in a finite number of steps, but when theoretically infinite sequences cannot be avoided we can approximate by cutting them off when we have reached sufficiently near to our goal.

These properties make computers by far the most powerful tool that man has ever had for handling information of all kinds. Their high speed, the low cost of a unit operation, their unwearying accuracy, and the virtually unlimited variety of what they can be programmed to do, allow them to compete with human capacities over a wide range of mental work, and thus to extend automation into 'white-collar' fields which were previously exempt from its challenge. Computers can also be programmed to act as subtle and resourceful automatic regulators which can, for instance, control a machine tool, a chemical processing plant, a telephone exchange or a power station, or direct the flow of traffic by road, rail or air. In these roles they intensify the competition that automation also presents to manual workers. Moreover, the advent of microcomputers, which combine very low cost with high reliability and portability, has now made automation economic at the level of an individual worker, whether in an office, a laboratory, a factory or a supermarket.

The increasing use of computers has coincided with a rapid expansion of national and international telecommunications. Over the same period the operations of businesses and governments have become more closely interwoven, and numerous international agencies and multinational corporations have been established. These developments have vastly increased the flows of data, and added greatly to the complexities of control. Much of the administration of government, and most of the management of business, now make extensive use of computers to collect, store, select and analyse data in order to extract the appropriate and timely information on which good decisions totally depend.

Industrial automation principally affects those who work - or who once worked - where it has been introduced, but office computer systems impinge directly on all of us as they prepare our bank statements and tax demands, compile and address the bills and circulars we unwillingly receive, control the restocking of our local shops, the issue of licences and so on. Most ordinary persons are well aware of the increasing use of computers for these purposes, and are eager to expound the consequences for themselves; their opinions are almost always unfavourable, in part for avoidable reasons which we shall consider later (chap. 4). The use of computers by research scientists is not commonly considered to be socially troublesome, but they are being used to accelerate the advance of science, for example in genetics and nuclear physics, and in the longer term this will have the most profound effects on the way we live, and on the ways in which we think about ourselves and the world around us.

None of these characteristics of computers should give us cause for despair; we should feel gratified that so powerful an instrument has been put at our disposal. When harmful consequences do come they flow from decisions and actions by those who use computers thoughtlessly or incompetently, or - much more rarely - with malign intent; they do not result from anything inherent in the machines themselves. This is so obvious that it ought not to need saying, but it is widely ignored. We must watch the men, not the machines, for what men will seek to do when exploiting computer technology is bound to affect the

4

life and work of everyone in an industrialized democracy. We need, therefore, to attempt to foresee and understand these changes, so that we can modify or moderate them should this be necessary to protect or to promote the interests of individuals and of society.

1.3 Prediction

Because our uses of computers are varied, important and widespread we must expect significant social consequences. We may hope to predict and prevent the more harmful of these, but even beneficial changes can be troublesome when they occur too rapidly. We must, therefore, attempt to predict not only what may happen, but also when and how fast. In computer technology the pace of change has been exceptionally rapid. Thus in a mere twenty years thermionic valves have given way first to transistors and now to the extreme miniaturization of 'large-scale integration'. Over the same period the operating speed has increased several hundredfold, and despite inflation the monetary cost of performing a set of typical operations has fallen by a factor of fifty or more. (In real terms, of course, the cost has fallen even more sharply.)

Prediction is an uncertain art. In its simplest form we take the past as a guide to the future, scrutinize it to detect trends, and extrapolate from them. This works reasonably well for the near future, since what is about to happen is for the most part determined by what equipment is already in production and available for use, what investments have actually been made, and what installations have been completed and commissioned. In any major new application of computers to business, industry or government, many years of planning and development work necessarily intervene between the initial conception and entry into full operational use. So long a time-scale introduces a measure of continuity which justifies the short-term extension of trends, especially when this is based on a knowledge of the commitments

5

and plans that have already been made.

To predict what may happen beyond the immediate future we have to deepen our understanding by going behind the trends and elucidating the factors that are causing the social or economic changes of interest so that we can evaluate their combined effects. This is especially necessary when we wish to deal with the dynamics of the situation in order to predict rates of change. Here, however, we meet two major difficulties which beset all social studies. First, there is the range and variability of human behaviour. It is easy to overlook the fact that the population of even one region is far from homogeneous, and that its characteristics are unlikely to remain fixed over the forecast period. The distribution of differences in age, sex, temperament, education, experience and economic class are all relevant when considering individual and social responses to change.

The second difficulty arises from the large number of simultaneously acting causes, and the complications that result because each may modify the influence of the others. Again, we rarely know which causes are effective in a given situation, or what is the precise form of the relation between them and the effects they produce. The picture is a confused one, somewhat like gardening where it is far from easy to discover which, if any, of several possible factors actually produced an improved crop. Social circumstances are, of course, even more complex, and not amenable to the controlled experimentation of horticultural research; multivariable analysis and other refined statistical techniques are therefore of limited value when preparing to analyse the contributions of computer technology to social change.

1.4 The assessment of technology

Concern about such unpleasing side-effects as pollution, noise, the depletion of natural resources and the consequences

of nuclear war has generated a public reaction against the un-
controlled introduction of new technology. It is no longer
acceptable to continue without some form of social control, and
it would be quite impracticable to abandon technology altogether
- as nostalgia occasionally suggests we should. A new proposal
can, therefore, expect to be required to satisfy social as well
as economic and technical criteria before it is judged to be
acceptable. In order to ascertain and evaluate its likely consequences procedures have been devised which are known as
'social impact analysis' or 'technology assessment'. Ideally,
these procedures should be carried out unemotionally and ob-
jectively, exploring all foreseeable side-effects, good as well
as bad, in order to make sure that no potential benefit or dis-
benefit is overlooked. The object is to enable alternative proposals, and remedial policies, to be compared rationally and
responsibly.

Various kinds of difficulty arise. First, we have those
related to the choice of social objectives; of what is to be
sought, and what avoided. Then, we have to decide over what
time-scale a proposal's effects should be examined. Objectives
involve values and these, with the timing of policy and action,
are major political questions on which the parties and interests
involved will probably hold quite diverse views. Nevertheless,
these issues cannot be fudged, for we cannot evaluate a given
change until we know whether it will carry us towards or away
from a declared objective. Moreover when comparing schemes we
need to estimate the extent of each retreat or advance, prefer-
ably on a scale that allows concurrent changes to be aggregated;
but many human and social benefits and disbenefits cannot be
quantified in any realistic way, and some attempts to calculate
'social costs' have had a very contrived air, and convinced few
but their authors.

Next, we are woefully ignorant of the fundamental con-
nexions between the causes of social change and the effects they

are presumed to produce. We rarely have well-established func-
tional relationships resting on a firm theoretical base, as we
do in the physical sciences, and so we frequently have to make
do with empirical correlations. This serious weakness, and the
inadequacy of the available data, together introduce great uncertainty into any projection into the future. Some of the relations we find are also difficult to handle, as for instance
when an effect has to rise above a threshold level for the public
to perceive it, or for its physical consequences to become
troublesome. Again, social and human behaviour responds in a
very complex manner to changes in circumstances, showing evidence of reaction, adaptation and initiative. None of this
makes for ease of analysis, but attempts are being made to design theoretical systems which reflect the principal characteristics of some human situation we wish to study. Such a system
can then be represented by a computer program that enables the
computer to act as a model of the real system. If we have sufficient insight to design our model to represent the dynamic
behaviour of our system as well as its steady states, then we
can use it to simulate many months or years of system behaviour
and evolution in a few minutes. Experiment with the model
allows it to be improved and refined, so that eventually it can
be used to give the best impression we can hope for of the effects of alternative policies, designs or parameters.

This reference to computer modelling indicates that the
assessment of technology can be expensive, and absorb a considerable amount of time and effort by expert staff. For these
reasons, it is important to decide very clearly at the outset
which aspects of a new technology are to be explored, over what
range of social activities and how far into the future. The
practical impossibility of making a complete study, and the
high cost of the multidisciplinary team needed to make an adequate one, explain why few assessments are made. Moreover, the
results are only more or less probable, and occasionally may

indicate adverse consequences that would not in fact arise. Nevertheless, it is important that technology assessments should be made: to clarify the social problems which exist, or which may arise; to guide decisions about social and economic problems and the allocation of resources; to educate public opinion and to inform governments.

Until such assessments are common their place will continue to be taken by the issue of soothing statements, such as

(a) the critics of the project are basing their alarmist remarks on mere speculation, for the alleged risks have not been proved to be serious (i.e. the future does not yet exist);

(b) such disadvantages as there might be would be limited and minor compared with the massive economic benefits to society in general (i.e. the unlucky few ought to be content to suffer for the fortunate many);

(c) the problems are only temporary, for the rapid advance of the technology will provide ways to reduce the harm (but, tomorrow's jam may bring its own unpalatable side-effects);

(d) should the social consequences unexpectedly prove to be stubbornly deleterious then the government will protect society by legislation (eventually, incompletely and in arrears, perhaps).

1.5 Computers and society

The social problems that our uses of computers are likely to raise are less obvious than those associated with some other technologies, for computing is not likely to destroy amenities or injure the physical environment. Computers do not themselves pollute the atmosphere or foul our rivers, nor do they generate excessive noise outside the computer room itself. Indeed, it could be claimed that communications between computers could reduce the conveyance of mail, and replace many human journeys, and so diminish the demand for travel, and reduce noise, pollution and the unnecessary consumption of energy. The other side of that coin is reduced employment in the transport and postal industries, and it is through this displacement of labour in a wide variety of tasks that computing seems likely to have its most immediate impact on men, women and society.

Economic effects may be initially the most troublesome, but the combination of computing and electronic communications is providing a very fast, world-wide information system which we must expect to have far reaching consequences. Political and economic power tend to reside near the sources of information, and computer-based information systems could be used to concentrate power. However, the technology really is neutral, and the development of cheap microcomputers could equally well be used to implement a policy of radical decentralization. The choice is ours - and it is a political, not a technical, one.

1.6 Bibliography

A general introduction to the concepts, terminology and uses of computers is given in

An Introduction to the Uses of Computers, by Murray Laver.
    Cambridge University Press, 1978.
More detailed accounts of computer techniques and technology appear in other volumes in this series, thus:
Information Representation and Manipulation in a Computer, by
    E.S.Page and L.B.Wilson. Cambridge University Press, 1973.
Computing Systems Hardware, by M.Wells. Cambridge University
    Press, 1976.
An Introduction to the Study of Programming Languages, by D.W.
    Barron. Cambridge University Press, 1977.
The problems and methods of forecasting are well discussed in
The Art of Anticipation, edited by S.Encel, P.K.Markstrand and
    W.Page. Martin Robertson, 1975.
The assessment of technology is reviewed in
Society and the Assessment of Technology, by Francois Hetman.
    O.E.C.D., Paris, 1973.

It and other aspects of the social control of technology are discussed in

The Politics of Technology, edited by Godfrey Boyle, David
    Elliott and Robin Roy. The Open University Press, 1977.

EXAMPLES 1

(1.1) List the characteristics of computers that are specially significant as causes of social change, and justify your choice.

(1.2) What factors impede the accurate prediction of social changes? How would you attempt to reduce their effects?

(1.3) 'Life never achieves a steady state: it is just one damned transient after another.' Explain why you disagree with this statement, or discuss its implications for social studies.

(1.4) Why are social impact analyses so rarely made?

(1.5) Criticize the concept of 'social costs'.

2 · Information and society

2.1 Information systems

The social changes likely to be stimulated by our use of computers will largely result from the increased availability of information of all kinds. Availability has two components: supply and selection. The supply of information is growing rapidly with the extension and continued improvement of telecommunication services; the selection of information is a task for computers. The electronic technology used in communications equipment is now virtually indistinguishable from that of computers. Operationally, also, computers use telecommunications to collect data for processing and to distribute results; and telecommunication systems use computers to control the switching centres (exchanges) that direct the routing of channels and messages. Communicating and computing are thus complementary functions in automatic information systems, and there is no longer much point in drawing a distinction between them.

Most of the time and money devoted to computing is spent on office work of various kinds. Traditionally, office work has been organized as a set of separate activities and skills: keeping accounts, maintaining records, accepting orders, ordering supplies, chasing progress, preparing invoices, and so on; but all of these are ways of producing the information that managers need to control the business. The computers that are used to perform these and other office jobs should, therefore, be regarded as components of business information systems. In some instances a conscious attempt has been made to design a 'management information system' to provide timely, accurate and comprehensive information in the hope that this would enable managers to reach better decisions. Often the designers of these systems were computer specialists with no first-hand knowledge of the business, and no personal experience of management, and they found it difficult to discover exactly what information was needed by the managers in their daily work, or what special circumstances might arise. Because of this, management information systems have only rarely responded adequately to all of the different needs of the various levels and functions of management.

One valuable feature of these systems, however, is that information which is used in several parts of a business is recorded once only and made available to all, rather than being held in a number of separate departmental files (which experience has shown may disagree). The central file is often called 'a common database', and it helps considerably to improve communications between the different parts of a large organization. The concept has been taken a stage further in the 'databanks' which provide for the shared use of information that is not confined to a single theme or to the affairs of one business - as in a general information system for public use.

Apart from conversation and other forms of private communication, our usual sources of information when we are not at work are newspapers, magazines, radio and television programmes and, for less ephemeral material, books and libraries. Each of these sources has three major limitations.

(a)   They present only what some author or editor has decided that 'his' public will be, or ought to be, interested in.

(b)   They are addressed to a wide-ranging audience or readership and are not, therefore, well matched to the specific capabilities and current needs of an individual recipient.

(c)   They make little or no provision for the return of questions, or for responding to requests for further information.

By using computer-controlled databanks we need not be limited in these ways. 'Viewdata' is the generic name of a major class of public information systems; in the United Kingdom, for instance, the viewdata service is operated by the Post Office under the name 'Prestel'.

2.2 Viewdata

Viewdata systems use public telephone networks to link individual customers to computers which give access to information held in central databanks. Each customer has a special 'terminal' which he can switch in to replace his telephone, and which has a keyboard for him to spell out his enquiries and a television screen on which the answers are displayed. When an enquiry is made, the appropriate computer in the system finds and returns the required information for presentation on the screen of the terminal. The range of search is narrowed in a kind of dialogue between the customer and the system: for instance, an enquiry might be initially defined as 'economic', and be progressively refined as 'financial', 'share prices', 'London Stock Exchange', 'Intergalactic Trading Corporation', and 'last ten day's closing prices'.

In principle, the volume of information that could be supplied by such a service is larger than it is convenient to handle in printed form, and very much larger than the tiny sample which it is practicable to broadcast in radio or television programmes. Moreover, there is no technical reason why an enquirer should not have access to the viewdata systems of any country in the world (although there are, of course, economic, and in some cases political, reasons that limit the range of enquiry). Editorial selection and author bias cannot be entirely eliminated, because someone has to decide what information should be in the databank, but their cramping and distorting effects can be much reduced, because an indefinitely wide range of material can be made available from alternative sources. Moreover, the enquirer is able to ask supplementary questions, and to select information in the quantity and at the level that he requires.

Viewdata services, however, have their own disadvantages. The amount of information that can be displayed at any one time on a terminal's screen is limited, and the effect is not unlike reading a newspaper through binoculars. Also, by presenting only what we have asked to see, the system prevents us from acquiring, by the happy accident of browsing, useful information which we did not know we needed. We have all learned as children to take in information by listening, reading a printed page and by watching television images. All of these we do without conscious effort, and none of them involves us in operating a machine (the terminal), which is an activity we associate with the skills of a trained technician. It will be interesting to see whether senior managers and administrators, for instance, accept and use viewdata terminals themselves, or whether they will regard this as a subordinate function, like typing, duplicating and filing. The first viewdata terminals to be installed in an organization may well be treated as status symbols, but once they become common they seem likely to be relegated to the outer office.

2.3 Some matters of policy

The provision and operation of a viewdata system requires economic and technical skills in computing and telecommunications; the input of information to its databanks is quite another matter. Viewdata provides an electronic publishing medium which, like the public telephone service, we expect to be available to anyone who will pay for its use, subject only to whatever restrictions apply to other media performing a similar function. For example, there could reasonably be restraints on the publication of pornographic, seditious or libellous material, or of personal information which infringes an individual's natural right to privacy. There could also be arguments about whether viewdata services should carry news or advertisements in competition with the newspapers and with broadcasting.

Those who are providing information to fill the viewdata-banks are, presumably, persons or organizations with information that they wish to make freely available to the public for their own reasons, or that they hope will earn them a fee each time it is sent to a customer's terminal. Hence the information available will be biassed towards announcements or 'propaganda', or to what someone believes will sell. For accounting reasons the system records the number of accesses to individual items of information, which makes it easy to identify those that earn the highest income; and the example of the press suggests that the range of items on offer may be limited to those that pay. There can be no guarantee that the information coverage will be complete; indeed this is unlikely unless there is some form of financial support from the government. Ought there to be a deliberate attempt to fill the gaps, and if so, which sections of the public should it aim to satisfy?

Further, viewdata presents itself to ordinary users as a simple extension of the public telephone system, which in most countries is owned, or closely regulated, by the state; and a number of questions arise: for example,

(a) Should viewdata customers be able to use the system's databanks to house their own private files of information?

(b) If so, should they be able to record messages in these files which they may permit others to read?

(c) If so, should these others be restricted to, say, the members of one business, or should the facility be more generally available as a form of electronic mail?

(d) Should the telecommunications authority be the monopoly provider of databanks and terminals as well as of the communication channels, or should there be competition between it and other operators: commercial, academic or public service?

16

(e) Should the telecommunication authority be itself a supplier of information - other than service information?

(f) Should viewdata be required to provide unrestricted access into other information networks, for example those with specialist databanks covering engineering, medical or scientific data at the professional level?

(g) Should computing services, also, be offered through the viewdata terminal, so that customers can process information drawn from the system's databanks - or, indeed, from any other source?

(h) If so, should these services be provided exclusively by the telecommunications authority, or should commercial computing bureaux be encouraged to sell their services through the viewdata terminal?

The general trend of these questions - and many other pertinent matters could be raised - is that there is no technical reason why viewdata should not itself become, or be interconnected with other systems to become, a comprehensive information, computing and correspondence service. Those able to afford to use viewdata would no doubt welcome and greatly benefit from such an extension of its capability, but it would raise serious economic and commercial problems for the privately owned suppliers of computer equipment and services, and for the postal and telex services. If for instance (b) were to be permitted but not the more open option of (c) then the operators of the viewdata system would need to be able to assure themselves that its rules were being observed by having the power to inspect the contents of users' data files, and to monitor the activity and identity of all who obtain access to them. This, even if it were to be done for the most inoffensive of commercial reasons, could look uncomfortably like the start of close surveillance by Big Brother.

Evidently public information systems raise a variety of difficult questions of policy, but there is no obvious single point where the separate parties involved are brought together to discuss them. On the provision side alone, we find computing, telecommunications, publishing, radio, television and public library interests; and the user side is totally diverse. We can regard this lack of a focal point as a weakness which carries the risk that no coherent policy will be formulated to guide the development of these systems, so that we may well drift wherever the tides of new technology and the strong currents of short-term commercial advantage happen to carry us. On the other hand, we can rejoice that the absence of central direction means that competition will be free to stimulate a speedy and flexible response to our needs as these reveal themselves. Experience suggests that it will probably generate new needs also.

On reflection we were, in fact, lucky not to have been saddled in the sixties with the costly provision of national 'computer grids', which were to have distributed raw computer power from large central machines. The able, and vocal, advocates of that policy argued that the economic advantages of using the largest available computers were sufficient to outweigh the diseconomies of distribution. The arguments slid rather easily over the inefficiencies of the software required to parcel out the central computers' power; and the advent of cheap microcomputers has now changed the entire basis of the calculation. We can confidently expect equally dramatic, and as yet unforseeable, changes in the technology of public information systems. It is therefore, important not to be committed too heavily, too finally, or too soon. Certainly, at the present time, users' requirements are too vague and information technology is changing too rapidly for anyone to know for certain what it might be best to do in the longer term.

2.4 The rich and the poor in information

The communication and computing services of a society can

be regarded as its 'nervous system', whose function it is to
tie together its institutions and its people, and to coordinate
their activities. Better and faster information services inevitably tend to encourage centralization and to promote uni-
formity, and these in turn make it easier to speed up and improve the services given, and so on. This cumulative process
could end in total control from the centre, an unpleasing prospect, and one that illustrates Marshal McLuhan's observation
that 'it is the framework itself that changes with new technology, and not just the picture within the frame'. There are,
however, no technological or economic imperatives that carry us
willy-nilly where we do not want to go. Even a technology as
powerful and pervasive as information technology is no more
than a tool for us to use to shape our future as we wish, provided only that we have the wit to decide and the will to act.

In considering what to do we need to recognize that our
existing social institutions have evolved for survival in an
environment where information was scarce and its distribution
far from uniform. Many examples could be given, but two will
suffice to illustrate the point. Success in business has been
based on acquiring earlier, fuller and more accurate information than one's rivals. The simultaneous availability of
economic and commercial information over a public system to all
who care to pay and enquire creates an entirely new situation;
for the market with perfect information exists only in the
earlier pages of economic textbooks. Then again, a similarly
universal access to the previous promises of an individual poli-
tician, and to his subsequent progress towards their achievement, would introduce a novel constraint into the conduct of
public affairs.

Clearly, we can expect an information-rich environment to
have considerable consequences, some of which we shall review
in later chapters. Of course, the environment will not be
equally rich for all. Some will not be able to afford to pay

to use their public information system, for a selective and comprehensive service cannot be cheap. Some will not be equipped by their education and experience to learn how to make full use of the service: they will neither know their needs, nor how to satisfy them. Some will simply not wish to spoil their heedless leisure with dry and dusty facts. Those who will benefit most are likely to be those who already benefit most from the services we have today, namely the eager, the ambitious and the competent.

The advance of information technology could thus make the information-rich even richer, and widen the gulf between them and the information-poor. This is a troublesome possibility because the information-poor will tend to be those who are also deprived economically and educationally, and who are thus most in need of the benefits that better information could bring. It seems likely that the provision of improved information services will be divisive between human and social groups, even though it is at the same time integrative between institutions and organizations. This argument can be extended to the international scene by substituting nations for individuals. It is possible that the development and use of computer-based information systems by the highly industrialized nations may, unintentionally but none the less effectively, increase the gap between their economic performance and those of the primary producers of the Third World. Such a result would not be conducive to peaceful co-existence.

2.5 Bibliography

The interactions between computers, communications and society are compactly examined in

The Changing Information Environment, by John McHale. Paul Elek, 1976.

The prospects for public information systems are considered in

The Information Utility and Social Choice, edited by H.Sackman and N.Nie. A.F.I.P.S. Press, 1970.

20

The human consequences of introducing computer technology into
the news media are the subject of
The Information Machines, by Ben H.Bagdikan. Harper and Row,
1971.
Among much other material, some details of American databanks
appear in
Information Technology in a Democracy, edited by Alan F.Westin.
Harvard University Press, 1971.
Background information about telecommunications appears in
Computers, Communications and Society, by Murray Laver. Oxford
University Press, 1975
which also discusses some of the policy questions raised by the
close relations between computing and telecommunication systems.
These questions are considered in an American context in
Computers and Telecommunications: Issues in Public Policy, by
S.L.Mathison and P.M.Walker. Prentice Hall, 1970
and a European view is presented in
*Computers and Telecommunications - Economic, Technical and
Organizational Issues*, by D.Kimbel. O.E.C.D. Informatics
Study No.3, Paris, 1973.

EXAMPLES 2

(2.1)   What are the advantages and disadvantages of
        (a) electronics,   (b) printing,
        for the distribution of information?
        Will electronic information systems make printed books
        and newspapers obsolete?
(2.2)   Compare and contrast viewdata systems with the 'teletext'
        services provided by the television authorities, for ex-
        ample Ceefax and Oracle in the United Kingdom.
(2.3)   Make a case for enacting legislation to limit competition
        between the viewdata and the postal services.
(2.4)   Indicate what factors or circumstances may limit the use-
        fulness of a common database for the managers of a large

business or organization.

(2.5)   'Public and other information systems using computers
will be socially and internationally divisive.'
Give your reasons for agreeing or disagreeing with this
statement.

3 · Some economic effects

3.1 Introduction

The most obvious, and certainly the most widely discussed, economic effect of using computers is on employment: it is important enough to merit a chapter on its own (see chap.4). There are, however, other effects such as those that arise in the collection and presentation of economic data, in economic analyses, and in the preparation of forecasts. All of these are relevant to the formulation of economic policies by governments and corporations, and in industrialized countries such as Britain and the U.S.A. the policies of these bodies impinge on our lives at many points, and extend their influences over a much wider range of activities than the production and consumption of goods.

3.2 Economics and its data

An ordinary reader of the lay press is bombarded with interpretations of events by amateur and professional economists. These commentators generally unite in their dislike for the economic policies of the government of the day, but their reasons for doing so often differ widely, and their analyses commonly lead to diverse proposals for remedial action. It seems that economists have not yet been able to formulate a major body of theory which is at once significant and universally agreed. Hence instead of one accepted science we have a number of competing schools. There is, perhaps, a link between their disagreements and the frailty of economic data.

Our word 'data' is a misleading one. From its origin and usage we might expect data to be facts which have emerged spontaneously and naturally out of the ordinary course of events in the world. In practice, however, we do not wait passively for facts to fall on our heads like Newton's apple. Nor are our data given to us; when we identify a need for information we set about collecting what we require, and we do so in ways that serve, and are coloured by, whatever purpose we have in mind. The best data result from observations or measurements that rest on a firm theoretical base. Until we have an acceptable hypothesis in which, say, quantities such as 'gross domestic product' or 'money supply' appear we have no reason to measure them, and no basis on which to define them with the precision we need in order to devise a method to do so. Nor can we judge what accuracy is relevant. Conversely if data are arbitrarily or imprecisely defined it is not easy to use them for developing and refining a satisfactory theory: this is often the case for data that have been collected for some quite different purpose in the past. Unfortunately even when they have been appropriately defined many economic data cannot be measured with much accuracy.

These points are made not to criticize the basis of economics, but to warn that the use of computers to process economic data can mislead the unwary by arousing unjustifiable expectations of accuracy and relevance. The computer user's traditional adage: Garbage In, Garbage Out (GIGO) reminds us that the results of computing, like those of cooking, can be no better than the ingredients, the recipe and the skill of the chef allow. When the data are uncertain and the theory insecure, reliable results are not to be expected no matter how excellent the programming may be. Refined statistical techniques can sometimes be used to reduce the effects of input error but theoretical weakness is more troublesome, for a tonne of computation cannot make up for the lack of a gram of insight.

3.3 The use of numerical data

Economic data serve to illustrate a more general point.

Quantitative facts are on the increase with the extending use of scientific methods, for science students are trained to share Lord Kelvin's prejudice for the precise, which he expressed by saying 'when you cannot express it in numbers, your knowledge is of a meagre and unsatisfactory kind'. It is somewhat carping to recollect that it was Kelvin who, in 1899, calculated the age of the Earth to lie between 20 and 40 million years; the geologists of his day argued in favour of a much longer period, and those of today have convincingly raised the figure to some 4600 millions. Expressing knowledge in numbers may make it less meagre, but it does not necessarily make it right. We do well to remember that qualitative knowledge comes first, and that in human affairs it is not to be despised.

The increasing use of computers, however, favours the quantitative rather than the qualitative, and we need to make two important reservations:

(a)   that the quantitative is not necessarily the more significant, only the easier to calculate with;

(b)   that measured numerical data are man-made; they do not occur naturally. It is, therefore, necessary to know precisely how the quantity in question was defined and for what purpose, when and where it was measured or estimated, by what method, how carefully and by whom.

Again, even when quantititave data are undeniably important it does not follow that measuring them with increased precision will add usefully to our information. The precision must always match the requirement: ± 1 gram is of no moment when weighing apples – but diamonds are different. One of the unfortunate consequences of using computers and electronic calculators is that, because they are designed to work with numbers of eight digits or more, their painless precision may induce the naive to believe that their results are equally accurate. When calculations required the labour of hand and brain no more digits were used than the occasion demanded.

3.4 Precision, accuracy and significance

In practice, three matters are commonly confused by those whose encounters with computers are infrequent or peripheral. They are precision, accuracy and significance. A simple, male chauvinist, example will show how they differ. A lady may announce with impressive precision that her age is $29\frac{3}{4}$, but experience suggests a somewhat lower accuracy and ±5 years is not significant anyway. In this example the social convention is well understood and no harm results. But the business pages of the more serious newspapers, and the official pronouncements of governments, continually publish economic and commercial data which have the appearance of great certainty and precision. The accuracies with which these statistics have been derived are rarely mentioned, but are often much less than their precision implies. Great care is necessary when using them in computation.

For example, it is customary in the industrial West for a nation to measure its vitality in terms of the rate of growth of its gross national product (GNP). This statistic is, therefore, regularly assessed and published, and its variations are matters of high concern and anxious debate. In Britain, the annual rate of growth of GNP has been around 3%, and it is usually quoted to one decimal place: thus 2.9% per annum. The official analysis of errors affecting the measurement of an individual value of GNP indicates that we can have no more than 90% confidence that the result is within ±3% of its true value. Hence, with an actual growth in a given year from, say, a nominal 100 to 102, the measured values would, at that level of confidence, lie somewhere in the ranges 100 ±3 and 102 ±3 so that the extreme ranges of the calculated growth would be (105-97) = 8% to (99-103) = -4%. The use of the decimal point seems rather futile therefore. Over so short a period as a year we cannot even know for certain whether the growth was positive or negative, yet its quarter-yearly variations are solemnly discussed.

It is a good rule to distrust any numerical fact that is

not accompanied by a statement of its likely error range. However, in favour of the use of computers in economics we may note that they allow vast amounts of tedious calculation to be performed quickly and cheaply, which enables us to repeat our calculations at intervals over the whole range of error of a given fact in order to test how sensitive our results are to its unavoidable uncertainty.

Accuracy, however, is not enough by itself; a fact needs also to be significant. Consider as an example the share indices published in many newspapers. Of these, the Dow Jones index summarizes a representative set of dealings on the New York Stock Exchange, and it is published daily with five-digit precision (thus 848.67). Over a year this index can vary by ±50, or more, and from day to day it fluctuates haphazardly by as much as ±15. There is no reason to doubt that the index is correctly calculated and is accurate to two places of decimals; but what meanings are its readers expected to attach to the fluctuations in the ±0.01 of its aptly named least significant digit? A useful rule is to consider what action you would want to take if the extreme right-hand digit of some published statistic were to vary by ±1; if none of any importance then lop off the right-hand digit; repeat this procedure, until the appropriate action becomes 'significant'. Under this treatment the Dow Jones index would probably lose two digits, and quotation to its nearest integer value (849) would be more rational. Other published share indices display similarly illusory precisions, and so do other more important economic facts.

We could dismiss the muddling of precision, accuracy and significance as a harmless aberration of the semi-numerate were it not that it confuses the interpretation of economic facts, and could stimulate counteractions by businesses and governments seeking to compensate for changes which either have not actually occurred, or which have little significance. When prestigious authorities publish figures that have been

generated by large and expensive computer systems we are apt to
assume that they would not have put themselves to so much
trouble and expense unless the results were accurate and important. Sadly, however, experience does not confirm this chari-
table expectation, and we do well to be wary. Of course, many
such figures are published to exhort rather than to inform; they
are statistical sermons, not scientific facts.

3.5 Computers and economic analysis

Economists have set themselves the enormously difficult
task of describing the behaviour of a very complex social system. Or at any rate they postulate that such a system exists,
for to do otherwise would be to abandon all hope of coherent
explanation and to fall back on mere historical description and
recording. Their principal problems are to decide what economic
quantities they should include in their system and what are to
be regarded as external to it, and then to specify with adequate
precision the relationships presumed to hold between the quantities. Computers can offer only supplementary help with these
problems, for their solution depends much more on the perceptive
formulation of hypotheses than on amassing and processing a
mountain of data. They can, of course, be used in the application of the powerful statistical tools developed for horticultural and industrial research, such as the analyses of variation and covariation, and these may help to indicate which
quantities are relevant and significant.

It is less common today for hypotheses to propose causal
mechanisms than to put forward mathematical statements which
describe the relationships between a number of variables. The
set of equations, or inequalities, used to express the behaviour
of some sector of economic activity is usually referred to as a
'mathematical model', or just a model, of it. When the activity
is simple, and the equations few in number, a pencil and paper
are the only tools required, but realistic situations require

many variables and large and unwieldy sets of equations. The
operation of a large economic model is most conveniently studied
by programming a computer to handle the corresponding calculations; indeed, it would often be quite impracticable to proceed in any other way. The computer has then been set up to
act as a simulator of the system, and the model is called, con-
fusingly, a 'computer model' meaning in this context a model
which *uses* a computer, and not a model *of* a computer.

The use of computers to drive economic models has a number
of advantages.

(a)   The models can be large enough to include as many variables and relationships as any economist is likely to be able
to handle.

(b)   They can handle non-linear, bounded, threshold, delayed,
feedback, probabilistic and other relationships which are difficult or impossible to deal with by formal analysis.

(c)   They can be processed repeatedly to reveal how sensitive
the result is to specific ranges of variation in input data, or
in the coefficients and constants in the relationships between
variables.   In this way an economist can experiment with his
surrogate system in order to develop and refine his ideas.

(d)   Except for black-box models, which merely describe the
overall relationships between input and output, we may hope
that our model's components and construction bear some resem-
blances to the factors operating in the real world.   To the extent that this is so the model will portray the system's dynamic behaviour as well as its static relationships, and it can
be used to reveal the transient effects which occur when conditions change.

(e)   As compared with purely verbal description and analysis,
the construction of a model forces the economist to state his
theses and assumptions precisely and unambiguously; and a model
also allows a much larger number of simultaneous interactions
to be evaluated than it is possible to handle in words alone.

29

Nevertheless, computer models have their disadvantages.

(i) Even the most complex model is a gross simplification of reality, and we can never be certain that every important factor has been included and given its proper weight.

(ii) By producing detailed results models help to foster the delusions of precision and certainty that we noted earlier. When our data are imperfect and our assumptions uncertain we can be just as wrong with a computer as without one.

(iii) It is almost impossible to check a model by retrodiction, that is by comparing the results it gives for some past period with what actually happened. Only rarely will adequate historical data exist, and when they do they will almost certainly have been used in devising the model itself, which makes them useless for checking it.

(iv) Even when a model does succeed in producing results that correspond encouragingly well with events, we have to remember that social values, goals and priorities change continually, so that future human behaviour will diverge more or less rapidly from the past on which the design of the model was necessarily based. Technological changes, also, will have substantial effects, but are notoriously difficult to predict. Moreover, so far as a model's results influence the thinking of economists, or the decisions of politicians, it will itself alter the future that we may wish it to predict.

(v) Models naturally appeal to theoreticians, but their combination of complexity with mathematics can confuse or repel those who are less academically minded, and thus reduce their practical value for business managers and government administrators.

(vi) Economic models rarely include political circumstances as a controlling variable, yet decisions about government expenditure, taxation policy or foreign affairs have major economic consequences.

The more closely a government seeks to control its economy and to manage social affairs the more predictable the future should become. It would, however, be fanciful to deduce the converse proposition and conclude that the use of computer models itself promotes the evolution of a managerial state. But, like other quantitative methods, the use of models is undoubtedly congenial to managerially minded politicians.

3.6 Computers and common sense

The general theme of this chapter is that computers, like all powerful tools, must be used with great care. We can easily allow ourselves to be dazzled by the apparent precision of numerical facts, and forget that there are more important objectives than merely maximizing the measurable. We can assume too readily that a computer's unbiassed accuracy also characterizes its results, forgetting that these depend wholly on the reliability, relevance and completeness of the input data, on the insight shown by the system designer, and on the care and skill of the programmer. Copernicus' hypothesis that the Earth moved around the Sun, although every day our experience plainly indicates the contrary, moved Galileo to admiration that men could so trust their reason as 'to commit such a rape on their senses'. We do not need to treat our common sense quite so roughly should it happen to challenge economic results issuing from a computer. Respectful scepticism is the proper attitude to all theoretical results - even the most scientific.

3.7 Bibliography

Wise comments on the fallibility of economic data are to be found in
On the Accuracy of Economic Observations, by Oskar Morgenstern.
Princeton University Press, 2nd edn. 1963
and also in
Wealth, by Charles Carter. Watts, 1968.
A modest example of the use of a model in forecasting appears in

Britain 2001 A.D., by Colin Leicester. H.M.S.O., 1972.
And the widely publicized world-model of The Club of Rome is
outlined and its results described in
The Limits to Growth, by Donella H.Meadows, Dennis L.Meadows,
Jorgen Randers and William Behrens III. Pan Books, 1974.
That model is criticized, and the limitations of modelling
generally are discussed by the Science Policy Research Unit of
the University of Sussex in
Thinking about the Future, edited by H.S.D.Cole, Christopher
Freeman, Marie Jahoda and K.L.R.Pavitt. Chatto & Windus,
1973
and also in
The Art of Anticipation, edited by Solomon Encel, Pauline K.
Marstrand and William Page. Martin Robertson, 1975.
No account of economic forecasting can ignore the dramatic
scenarios painted by the surprise-free predictions of the staff
of the Hudson Institute in
The Year 2000, by Herman Kahn and Anthony J.Wiener. Macmillan,
1967
and in
The Next 200 Years, by Herman Kahn, William Brown and Leon
Martel. Associated Business Programmes, 1977.

EXAMPLES 3

(3.1)   Write notes on the sources of error and bias in published
economic data.
(3.2)   Kelvin wrote that knowledge which cannot be expressed in
numbers 'is of a meagre and unsatisfactory kind'. Give
your reasons for agreeing, or disagreeing, with his
statement.
(3.3)   What do you understand by an economic model?
(3.4)   List and comment on some examples of illusory precision
in published economic data.
(3.5)   An advertisement for an electronic clock states that it

will keep time to better than '60 seconds per year', and it implies that this accuracy derives from the fact that its quartz crystal vibrates with a frequency of 4194304 cycles per second. Comment on the relevance of that fact, and on the validity of the implication.

4 · Computers and employment

4.1 Computers and productivity

No one sets out with the deliberate intention of using a
computer to create unemployment. The prime objectives in most
commercial and industrial applications of computers have been
to increase efficiency and to secure economies. Each of these
contributes to reducing the unit cost of producing something,
or of providing some service. When it is a matter of over-
heads, or the civil service, almost everyone speaks out fear-
lessly in favour of cutting costs. In other fields, however,
when managements decide to initiate cost-cutting projects they
find it prudent to present these as ways of increasing 'productivity'. That disarming word makes it seem churlish or irrational to oppose so obviously desirable an objective. However, we need to be clear that 'lower unit costs' and 'higher
productivity' are alternative measures for what is essentially
the same thing.

Productivity - the ratio of output to input - is an index
which can be calculated for the use of any resource which is
consumed in creating a product or a service. Thus we can speak
of the productivity of using a raw material, or of an item of
capital equipment, but when the word is used without qualifi-
cation it refers to the use of labour. For example, the productivity of miners may be expressed in 'tons of coal per man-
shift', or of typists in 'key-depressions per hour'. Experience has shown that almost all successful policies for increases in labour productivity have resulted from technological
advance. They have rarely required any more physical effort,
and they have usually reduced the degree of skill required
- often to a trivial level. Typically, they have involved

investment in equipment of a new design which could be operated
by a smaller work force to produce a larger output: the classi-
cal substitution of capital for labour. For these reasons productivity has increased most in prosperous industries with expanding markets.

The characteristics of computers that allow them to be
used to increase productivity are their high speed, low operating costs, and the programmability which enables them to act
as automatic control mechanisms of great power and subtlety.
Their programming also gives computers a versatility that enables us to apply them to the control of a wide variety of industrial processes and plant, ranging from an oil refinery to
a single machine tool. With some cost and effort computers
can be programmed to handle a much broader range of conditions
and contingencies than any unaided human operator, and to respond very rapidly to changing circumstances or needs. They
can also optimize the adjustment of the plant or process continuously, and relieve men and women of dirty, dangerous and
tedious tasks. As well as increasing productivity, computer
control can detect the onset of potentially dangerous conditions, and initiate action to protect the plant against damage or failure. Thus the investment needed to provide computer control in a large power station is relatively small,
and it would be more than recovered if it were to prevent just
one unscheduled shutdown in the station's entire working life.

4.2 Productivity and employment

It is an obvious fact, but one that is often overlooked or
glossed over, that an increase in productivity implies a decrease in employment unless output can be increased in at least
the same proportion. Output can be increased only if sales are
also increased, and those who launch productivity improvement
schemes do so in the hope that by reducing their unit production
costs they will be able to reduce their selling price and thus

increase sales by tapping new markets. Such a happy outcome is not possible where an increase in total sales is not feasible. They may then merely undercut their competitors, and 'transfer' unemployment to them. The headquarters of a business or a government department may not need to produce any more letters or reports - may even be seeking to reduce their number - but will install a computer-controlled word-processing system to reduce office costs by saving the salaries of the typists who will be displaced, or of those additional ones it will not need to employ.

In the same way, the numbers of journalists and compositors employed in a newspaper office bear no simple relation to the number of copies sold. Their output is one copy of the text and the set-up type for the printing presses. By the use of computer-controlled typesetting machines, which the journalists can operate directly, the need for compositors can be very substantially reduced, and in a number of countries proposals to install these machines have generated severe and stubborn problems of industrial relations. This example illustrates rather starkly that the concept of productivity is not always appropriate, for when a stage in a production process is eliminated the productivity of its workers rises to infinity as their number falls to zero! The employer and the community may benefit from such a change, but we should not be too surprised to find that those who are made redundant take a more parochial view.

One result of the use of computers has been that automation, which in its earlier forms affected only manual workers, was suddenly extended to a wide range of white-collar employees. The lower levels of office work - simple accounting, stock control, ordering, progress chasing, personal records and so on - involve little more than routine tasks which can easily be programmed and transferred to computer systems. The more straightforward aspects of professional work - simple engineering design, some draughting and mapping, statistical analysis and tabulation, for instance - can also be codified and encapsulated in standard computer programs. This industrialization of their work has altered the approach of many white-collar staff to their employment, and inclined them to adopt the forms and procedures evolved by manual workers. Thus we have seen the replacement of gentlemanly 'staff associations', limited to a single firm, by abrasive white-collar unions organized on a national scale, and independent of all employers. Whereas industrial action by 'the staff' was once unthinkable, it has become 'normal'; and although the introduction of computers into offices may not have been the sole cause, it has undoubtedly helped to accelerate this significant social change.

Opinions are divided about the effects of computers on employment. The trade unions tend to be pessimistic and conservative. They see computers as a threat, and tenaciously remember every case where jobs were lost. For their members, new technology is summed up in four Rs, redundancy, redeployment, retraining and reduced skills. They fear computers also, as a disruptive force which can destroy their painfully established negotiating positions overnight by disturbing relativities and devaluing skills, and by creating new groups of workers whose allegiance may more properly belong to another union, or to no existing one. It is easy to criticize these attitudes as sullen Luddite opposition, or as a temporizing expediency which may save some jobs in the short term only to lose them and more in the long term as more progressive competitors steal their employers' markets. They may, however, be just a preliminary stance from which the union hopes to negotiate concessions in return for its members' acceptance of innovation.

On the other hand, those engaged in the manufacture, programming and operation of computers point to the many thousands of entirely new jobs which these activities have created, and to the opportunities that lie ahead. Some users of computers,

also, argue that by increasing their competitiveness computers
have helped them to stay in business and continue to provide
employment. Increased productivity is economically necessary
but rising unemployment is socially unacceptable, and the rising
level of production needed to escape between the horns of that
dilemma has proved difficult to achieve. No developed country
dare refrain from using computers, for its international competitors will not do so and, unless it were to impose restraints
on foreign trade, imports would rapidly undercut and displace
home production causing business failures and unemployment. It
is more than likely that we have neither the facts nor the understanding to be able to predict the long-term effects of computers on employment, but short-term increases in unemployment
and enforced changes of job seem inevitable, as they are with
most changes in technology.

4.3 Microcomputers, automation and employment

Until the advent of the microcomputer, computers came in
rather large units of power and cost, which tended to limit
their application to large-scale operations, and to the more
prosperous firms. These were often those whose business was
expanding, so that productivity gains could be offset against
increasing output, and redundancies were limited. The fact
that expansion produced a less than proportional growth in the
number of jobs would be known to few inside these companies,
and probably to no one outside. The effect of computers in
reducing employment has thus developed more slowly than was
feared.

Microcomputers are reliable, portable and cheap enough to
be incorporated in instruments, tools and other devices for
use by an individual worker - whether typist, architectural
draughtsman, service engineer, supermarket cashier, or whatever. For this reason some believe that they pose a major
threat to employment, and one which will develop rapidly.

However, the economics of microcomputer production require very large runs of standard units. For the hardware itself, high fixed-costs are incurred in designing and in setting up a production line, and large volumes are needed to bring down the unit price. A more troublesome constraint is the high cost of designing, producing and proving a program, and because this is very largely a labour cost it will rise as the salaries of systems analysts and programmers continue to rise.

For each new application, therefore, programming imposes a high fixed-cost, and it is possible that microcomputers will find their principal sales where standardized mass-market applications are easy to locate and satisfy. For instance, microcomputer-controlled locks opened by a personal code, chosen by the user and changed at will, could have as much impact on the lock business as did quartz watches on another traditional industry. Standard mass markets are to be found in domestic uses, in instrumentation, in controls for automobiles, in such office equipment as word processors and duplicators, and in devices for use in retail selling. The first three of these should have little or no adverse effect on employment; indeed, they could even increase it by enlarging the range of products offered to tempt the mass consumer. The last two suggest that the microcomputer may have its principal effect on employment in the service industries. If so, that would be a rather significant result, for some economists believe that the developed countries are moving from an industrial to a post-industrial phase in which most of the working population will be employed in providing services rather than in manufacturing goods. It would be serious indeed if the use of microcomputers were to curb the service industries' demand for labour just when it was hoped that their expansion would absorb the workers which automation is displacing from manufacturing. Perhaps we should concentrate on developing personal attitudes and social norms which will create a demand for those forms of personal service

that are not suitable for automation because they require
uniquely individual attention.

4.4 Employment and social change

The change from an agricultural to an industrial society
followed the development of power tools and the mechanization
of manufacturing. More recently, automatic controls were extended to enable several successive stages in the manufacture
of a product to be completed without human intervention. This
phase, known as automation, is greatly assisted by computers,
and it is most readily applied to continuous processes, such as
the production of steel, cement, glass, paper and petrochemi-
cals. In the next phase, which is just beginning, computers
will control industrial manipulators, sometimes called robots,
which will be equipped with a variety of measuring and sensing
devices, and with the mechanical equivalents of arms and hands.
These robots will be programmed to hold materials in the correct
positions for machine tools to work on; they will also control
the tools and move items from tool to tool as the work pro-
gresses. The essential difference between this phase and conventional automation is that the production line, with its
tools and robots, will be less 'product-specific'; that is, it
will not be designed and constructed to suit a single product.
It will thus be possible to use the same line to manufacture a
range of different - but not totally dissimilar - products simply by changing the robots' control programs and the raw materials. Needless to say, the robots will be functionally designed and will look like rather dull machines, and not at all
like the glamorous androids of science fiction; nor will they
be 'intelligent' in the true sense of that much misused word.

The social changes produced by the move from agriculture
are recorded in numerous histories of the industrial revol-
ution; and the earlier phases of automation carry that story
into the twentieth century. Industrialization was based on

40

the 'division of labour' in which the skilled work of individual craftsmen is replaced by a sequence of simple operations each performed by semi-skilled machine operatives. This de-skilling, plus the facts that an operative rarely produces an identifiable output or is allowed to make decisions that influence the conduct of the work, destroy the satisfaction that a craftsman derives from work well done. The result may be a sense of detachment, or even alienation, from the work; and a job becomes merely someone's current way of earning money.

Alienation has spread from the factory floor to many office workers as their work has been deskilled, paced, monitored and generally downgraded when a computer was introduced. This is especially likely when an insensitively designed system leaves the staff feeling that the computer is using them merely to supply its input, rather than that they are using the computer to assist them in their work. The 'staff' of a company used to identify themselves with its aims and objectives, but they now tend to have a less committed approach to their employment. Some react to this situation by advocating a return to a simpler, even a rural, life style, but it would be unrealistic to suppose that developed urban societies will abandon innovation. It would be valuable, therefore, to encourage employees to acquire the understanding they need in order to cooperate in the design of systems which have so much effect on their working lives.

We should note at this point that there is nothing inherent in computer technology that requires automation or robotics to develop in the way that they have. Data can be transmitted to and from computers over the public telephone network, and computers can be linked together to share each other's data and results. Microcomputers are cheap enough to be used to control small-scale manufacturing and service operations. In principle, we could disperse some of our large factories, and most of our large offices, in order to allow men and women to

41

work together in small groups established in the suburbs, small town and villages where they live. These operations could be linked together for the purposes of coordination and control - and, in the case of offices, for the receipt and delivery of work - by transmitting data to and from headquarters, and yet leave a large measure of autonomy in local hands. We have, however, much to learn about the design of dispersed computing systems before these can be fully effective and economic.

The social merits of such a dispersed approach are obvious, and the economic penalties need not be too high; they might in any event be lower than those of alienation. We *could* decide to proceed in some such fashion to give automation a more human face, but history records few examples of a centre willingly dispersing its power to the periphery. Nevertheless, the technical means exist, and they challenge us to use them.

4.5 System design for service, or efficiency?

Computers and automation are loved by few. In part, this low esteem reflects a general distrust of high technology. In part, however, it has been generated by some striking examples of naive and inappropriate design of computer systems, by an insensitive clumsiness in putting them into service, and by journalists' delight in reporting the more bizarre examples. These faults can and should be corrected. Computer specialists usually have had no previous experience of the tasks which their systems will be used to perform; nor are they necessarily good at the management of men or projects. Their skills are those of computing, and specialists are noted (and paid) for the depth of their knowledge, not the breadth of their understanding.

Up to now, design has been dominated by the hot pursuit of efficiency and economy, and there has been no pay-off in merely avoiding or reducing other people's dissatisfaction. Human factors have commonly been treated as tiresome limitations to be designed around, or even out of the system, whereas the design should respond totally to human needs and capabilities. It is, therefore, highly desirable that all who will be affected by a proposed computer system should be closely involved in its planning and design. They cannot be expected, nor will most of them wish, to settle the technical details of the equipment or its programming; but they have an indispensable contribution to make to the much more fundamental tasks of determining precisely what the system should do, what objectives should be pursued, and what methods and time scales should be used in bringing it into service. Only thus can we be reasonably sure that the system will satisfy real needs. This is not to criticize the competence or the motives of computer specialists; but their own professional criteria are those of efficiency and technical elegance rather than human relations, or the promotion of job satisfaction.

Obviously it would be wholly impracticable to consult everyone who might be affected by a new computer system, and we have to devise a way of working through the use of representatives. For the workers themselves, their trade union representatives may seem to be the natural choice, but trade unions have not evolved to fulfil this kind of function. They have developed to defend and improve their members' pay and working conditions, and their role has been critical and conservative rather than creative and innovatory. However, the trend towards the wider participation in management implied by 'industrial democracy', seems likely to enlarge the unions' horizons, and to stimulate them to develop their own information needs which they will expect to be included in the design of commercial computer systems.

Then there are those whose dealings with a business as its customers may be affected by a new computer system. Some public corporations (the Post Office for example) already have consumer or user councils which could provide suitable machinery. For others the choice and appointment of representatives could present difficult problems, unless local councillors or MPs could be persuaded to act. It would be foolish, however, to allow the lack of a perfect solution to delay the initiation of a more participative approach to systems design. Only thus can we hope to dispel the distrust and dislike engendered by the use of computers, and to ensure that they serve – and are seen to serve – the real needs of ordinary people. It should be noted that some see all such proposals for wider participation as mere devices for 'protest absorption'; and they castigate efforts to humanize work as the practice of a 'cow sociology' intended to quieten and induce a placid state of mind. They argue that these are conscious attempts to distract workers from demanding a much more radical reconstruction of the economic basis of society. Such conspiracy theories are not confined to the right or to the left in politics.

4.6 Work sharing

No law of nature or economics requires a man or woman to work for 40 hours a week, 50 weeks in the year, for 45 years. Hence when productivity rises faster than sales it would be possible to offset the effect on employment by reducing the working week, increasing holidays or by earlier retirement. This approach does not appeal to employers intent on reducing costs, for unless wages were reduced there would be a rise in labour costs. Their purpose is better served by employing fewer workers for longer hours, and in working shifts to earn the maximum return on the use of expensive capital equipment. The historical trend, however, has been to shorten the working week, which for industrial workers has shrunk from 65 to 40 hours over the last century or so.

If the use of computers, with other technological advances, were to generate rising levels of unemployment, the governments might decide to attempt to reduce these by sharing around the work to be done. Putting such a policy into execution would require a number of social changes. For example:

(a) It would reduce or abolish overtime earnings, which are a significant, and cherished, component of many workers' wages.

(b) It would involve some measure of central planning and direction of labour.

(c) It would require a flexible redeployment of labour which implies

    (i)   increased mobility, with its considerable consequences for schools and housing;

    (ii) movements between employers and skills that would require trade unions to refrain from demarcation disputes, and to accept unpredictable fluctuations in membership and negotiating strength;

    (iii) the coordination of wage scales to a degree that would disturb existing patterns of differential payments and relativities;

    (iv) substantially increased retraining.

None of these changes is impossible, but none of them could happen quickly, or without creating industrial turbulence.

4.7 Bibliography

A classic, but far from obsolete, essay on automation in relation to men and women is

The Human Use of Human Beings, by Norbert Wiener. Sphere Books, 1968.

The alienation produced by industrialization and automation is examined in

Problems of an Industrial Society, by William A.Faunce. McGraw Hill, 1968.

The social consequences of moving on from the manufacture of goods to the provision of services are explored in

The Coming of Post-Industrial Society, by Daniel Bell. Penguin Books, 1976.

Contributions on participation in the planning and control of
technology are presented in the Open University's reader,
The Politics of Technology, by Godfrey Boyle, David Elliott
and Robin Roy. Open University Press, 1977.

EXAMPLES 4

(4.1)   'Computers are having more significant effects on office
staff than on factory workers.'
Explain why you agree, or disagree, with this statement.

(4.2)   Define productivity, and comment on its applications and
relevance to

(a)   the manufacture of biscuits,

(b)   the manufacture of Rolls Royce cars,

(c)   the painting of a portrait,

(d)   digging and immediately refilling holes in the
ground,

(e)   carrying out scientific research,

(f)   carrying out market research.

(4.3)   Discuss the pros and cons of work-sharing as a means of
reducing unemployment.

(4.4)   Examine the merits and disadvantages of dispersing manufacturing and office work into small units able to operate with the minimum practicable amount of central coordination.

(4.5)   Assuming that it is desirable for those affected by the
operation of a new computer system to participate in its
design, discuss the problems that this presents.

5 · Education and leisure

5.1 Introduction

Our expanding use of computers is changing working methods
and skills at an increasingly rapid rate, and we will all need
to be better prepared by our education than we have been to accept and adapt to these changes. We will need also to be re-
trained at intervals until we stop working. As productivity
increases through the use of computers, and in other ways, we
can expect consequential increases in leisure, either as a deliberate social policy, or because we have failed to achieve
sufficient economic growth.

These developments could require considerable changes to
be made in the content, aims and timing of public education.
At the level of technique, also, computer systems are being
developed to assist teaching and learning in the classroom and
outside. Microcomputers are finding direct uses in the 'leisure
industry' as they are being applied to games, gambles and a
variety of standardized amusements designed to fill the time
vacated by work.

5.2 Education, work and computers

In the early part of this century the son of a craftsman
could enter the same trade and expect to use the same tools and
techniques as his father had used throughout his working life.
Today, the pace of technological development continues to accelerate and the interval between significant changes in working
practice, already much less than a lifetime, is continuing to
decrease. In the words of Margaret Mead: 'no one will live all
his life in the world into which he was born, and no one will
die in the world in which he worked'. Few of us, indeed, will

spend the whole of our working lives practising a single set of skills. The recurring demand for new skills will mean that all of us will need periodic retraining, and our lives may come to resemble a series of sandwich courses, in which our education and training is distributed in slices throughout our active years, instead of being concentrated into one thick slab at their beginning. How thin the slices can be will depend on the nature of the job, and on the training methods employed. Some skills will become obsolete sooner than others. Routine operations in an insensitively designed system will require very little skill, and no more than a few hours training on the job. More worthwhile jobs, planned to provide satisfying work as well as increased productivity, will require much longer periods of training. We can expect to see an increased use of computers as teaching aids; indeed, a computer system could be designed to serve as its own training aid, and to instruct its operators either initially or as a refresher course. To do this it would first disconnect the operator's controls from the actual production operation and then simulate the occurrence of a variety of normal and abnormal conditions in order to monitor the operator's responses and comment on their relevance. Some operators would find this helpful and stimulating, but others might resent it as a form of close surveillance and appraisal.

Technical education, in particular, will need to change by cutting itself free from current practices and skills, for these are doomed to increasingly early obsolescence. Those employers who still urge that education should concentrate on vocationally relevant skills are short-sightedly focussing on the immediate situation, and failing to foresee what will be their own long-term requirement. All education, technical and general, must seek to provide students with a broad and solid foundation of fundamentals on which their future training and retraining can be built. To use Robert Hutchin's splendid paradox: 'the most practical education is the most theoretical one'; certainly no other can provide as enduring a base. It may also be necessary to go beyond retraining, and provide for longer and less specialized periods of re-education in order to consolidate and extend people's basic knowledge in preparation for subsequent stages in their working lives. Sabbatical years may cease to be an academic privilege, and become the norm; if so, they would also occupy some of the time set free by increased productivity.

5.3 The problem of leisure

For many the prospect of increased leisure is an unalloyed good, but for others it is just so much more empty time to fill or kill. Indeed, there is evidence that in many instances the shortening of the standard working week has not in fact reduced the number of hours spent at work. For some, more of these hours are now paid at overtime rates, and the shorter working week is a cosmetic disguise for higher pay. Others have taken up 'moonlighting', and use their free time to work at a second job, once again to increase their income. Yet others, faced with the rising costs of personal and domestic services of all kinds, have taken to decorating and maintaining their own houses, growing their own vegetables and to performing other chores which at one time they might have paid others to do for them. In each of these cases the earning or saving of money has been preferred to the enjoyment of leisure.

It was suggested in the previous chapter that automation has tended to diminish the sense of achievement that its operatives gain from their work. In extreme cases this may lead to a state of 'alienation' in which work becomes an unavoidable evil - a way of earning money - and the worker disconnects himself from all personal involvement in it. Those who fail to find satisfaction or any sense of purposeful activity at work may well switch to seeking these in outside pursuits where their individual contributions are visible, and recognized by those whose respect they value. What they do in their leisure time then becomes the most important aspect of their lives, and the one which connects them to society and gives them a role and status in it.

Many people, however, have no such consuming interest to fill their leisure, and for them free time merely becomes a tiresome vacancy in which they are idle and bored. Unfortunately this may be true of those who are most likely to be made redundant by automation, who are least prepared by their education for either work or leisure. Obviously, also, it is worse when someone is unemployed - or has never been employed. Alienation at work combined with boredom at home is a recipe for social unrest, especially among the energetic young. How then, ought they to attempt to fill the leisure which computer-propelled productivity may force upon them?

'Ought' is, of course, a normative word which, with such phrases as 'the right use of leisure', has overtones of Victorian do-goodery. It implies that some uses of leisure are better than others; for example, that it is better to read the classics of literature than to look at the comics, or that it is better to play chess in a club than darts in a pub. There is an implication that it is better to be active than passive, better to play bad football than to watch professional matches on television. Those that hold these views argue that neither primary nor higher education does anything like enough to prepare us to fill our leisure in 'worthwhile' ways; and they commend all forms of adult education, from evening classes in woodwork to Open University degrees in biophysics. On the other hand, critics note that there is no evidence that those who pursue intellectual or aesthetic activities are happier or more socially useful than others. More politically minded critics even dismiss such proposals as 'élitist' or 'paternalistic', for they see them as condescending attempts to direct the free activity of responsible adult men and women as if they were children, or as crafty ploys to distract discontented workers from planning social change.

Clearly any discussion of the use of leisure is made more difficult by the lack of a common set of values in contemporary society. Many reasons have been suggested for this, ranging from the decline of religion to the effects of war. Computer technology may itself have helped in recent times because, being value-free, its criteria are technical and economic. Its practitioners have adopted these same criteria when designing computer systems, with the unhappy result that their absolute rationality, and their emphasis on quantitative data and results, have devalued qualitative facts and emotional needs by ignoring them. It is not surprising that the great prestige of science in the recent past should have led to some neglect of human virtues and values, for science's objectivity and universality derive from its rigorous exclusion of subjective data. Hence when using any science-based technology we must take pains to ensure that we do not overlook human needs, for we all too readily relapse into considering only those requirements that fit conveniently into a numerical framework. This warning applies with special emphasis to our use of computers, because these are machines of great generality whose influence is permeating many aspects of our lives - and not only those related to industry, commerce and government.

Perhaps the only value judgement that is likely to find wide acceptance is that individual men and women are important in their own right; few regimes or ideologies openly deny that view. We may, therefore, conclude that it is reasonable to equip people to be able to realize their own potential, whether at work or at leisure, so that they can avoid declining into the sad syndromes of listlessness or alienation. Our education ought to give us at least the basic tools we need for that purpose; above all it must equip us to learn, and to exercise an independent critical judgement. This last would help to counter the high-powered presentation by the media of the commercial stereotypes of wealthy-leisured-class behaviour as if they were models worthy of our emulation.

5.4 Computer-assisted instruction

A great deal of work has been done to apply computers to the processes of teaching and learning. A computer can readily supply information to a remote terminal which has a keyboard for the asking of questions, and a screen for displaying answers. In order to cater for the blind, adaptations are necessary, and it should soon be possible to speak questions, probably in a limited and standardized vocabulary and format, and be answered by a synthetic voice. A large computer can handle independent requests from an hundred or more terminals at the same time, and provide each with a rapid, selective and individual information service. As we have seen, viewdata systems (chap.2) are examples of public information services of this kind.

A computer can take a more active part in instruction by the use of 'programmed learning'. This method is well suited to computers, but is not specific to them; specially printed books can also be used. In brief, when a computer is used in pro-grammed learning the pupil sits at a terminal on which tutorial information is displayed, followed by questions designed to test his understanding. Answers submitted through the keyboard are checked by the computer, and as long as they remain accu-rate more information is presented, and instruction proceeds. Incorrect answers are analysed, and the program returns the pupil to an earlier point where the forgotten or misunderstood information is presented again in its original form, or in an-other designed to cater for the difficulty revealed by the pupil's answer. Revision tests can be set at longer intervals, and the pupil referred back as necessary. As well as helping a pupil to learn, the system can keep a record of his progress and of the difficulties encountered and overcome.

The advantages claimed for computer-assisted instruction include the following:

(a) each pupil receives individual and private instruction;

(b) pupils proceed at their own pace, and at times convenient to them;

(c) the computer is supremely patient, ready to return a dozen times to the same point without irritation or sarcasm;

(d) the pupil is not distracted by the troublesome problems of human interaction in the classroom: mutual antipathy, favouritism, indiscipline and so on;

(e) the course material and methods can be prepared by the best teachers of the subject and made available to all.

On the other hand:

(i) no machine can replace the inspiration given by a gifted teacher;

(ii) no program can foresee and provide for every problem that will arise in use;

(iii) some people dislike machines, or lack confidence when using them;

(iv) the use of a computer is a seductive and insidious way of conditioning students to accept a technological culture;

(v) computer-assisted instruction greatly increases the opportunities for propagating a single point of view because the high costs of production favour the universal use of the 'one best' program.

Whatever its merits in general education, computer-assisted instruction could enable us to study at home in our own time, either to occupy our leisure, or to acquire background information related to some leisure interest. In Britain, the Open University was intended to introduce a new factor into higher education, and it would be possible to extend its principle downwards to 'Open Colleges', perhaps organized regionally, by making courses available over viewdata systems. Although such

a development is technically possible it may cost more than we
are prepared to spend at present. Nevertheless, it serves to
show that the use of computers could be a major agent of social
change in the politically sensitive, but economically important,
field of education.

5.5 Computer arts and crafts

The arts and crafts are leisure activities respected for
the skill they require, and are recommended as a therapy to
dispel boredom and relieve the stresses of our working lives.
At first sight they may seem to be far removed from connexion
with computers, although intrepid men and women have from time
to time programmed computers to write music and poetry, and to
paint and draw. However, no work has yet appeared which has
been acclaimed by the art or music critics, and certainly not
by literary ones. The programs use the basic rules of the art
to guide and control the computer's output, and rely for their
creative invention on some weakly controlled or random process
to generate a stream of undetermined results. These are then
filtered to reject those that fail to satisfy whatever criteria
the programmer has chosen to incorporate. The problem is not
to create unexpected, or undetermined output, but to select
the tiny fraction of it that may have some slight pretension
to artistic merit.

Computer art is one thing; computer-assisted art is quite
another and much less developed field. Computers are already
driving machines which draw coloured graphs, diagrams and maps,
and most university computer centres display decorative tracings
produced by playful programmers and ingenious mathematicians.
It would be easy to use a microcomputer to assist an operator
to produce patterns and abstract displays – static or dynamic –
on the screen of a colour television receiver. The computer
would do the donkey work of interacting with the receiver's
electronics. It would also supplement the operator's skill

by generating and fitting together on demand straight lines, regular or irregular polygons, arcs of circles or ellipses, segments of parabolas, hyperbolas and so on. Or again, in music a microcomputer could, perhaps, be used to provide a simple keyboard control for the more difficult instruments, and thus reduce the level of skill required to begin to play. Rather obviously, a computer can control an electronic synthesizer able to simulate the tonal qualities of traditional instruments. In such a fashion it should be possible to cater for people who, although they may differ greatly in competence, are equally in need of the benefits of creative activity. One group in special need of help are the mentally or physically handicapped, and microcomputers would have produced a significant social gain if they were used to enable them to share more fully in the pleasures of executant performance in music and the graphic arts.

5.6 Games and other amusements

We have a great capacity for developing a splendic technology and then wasting it on inane frivolities. The microcomputer will certainly not avoid that folly, for it will be applied to the control of one-armed bandits, pin tables and the other appurtenances of amusement arcades. Preprogrammed electronic games, using the domestic television screen, are already on sale, and it is confidently predicted that they will provide a large and expanding market. Indeed, the size of the installed capacity for the production of microelectronic devices makes this one of those self-fulfilling prophecies.

Chess has attracted a considerable amount of attention from computer scientists. In part, this is because its complexity ensures that it is impracticable to program a computer to play by a complete enumeration and evaluation of every legal move. Chess-playing programs have, therefore, made use of strategies appropriate to the principal stages of the game. Work on them has paralleled work on systems designed to exhibit some aspects of what would be called intelligent behaviour in a human being; and it has provided a pleasant and stimulating diversion from the rigours and frustrations of that work. Chess-playing programs have now reached the standard of very good club players, but are not yet quite able to beat a grand master. Preprogrammed microcomputer-controlled chess games are on sale, and play well enough to amuse a beginner.

It is conceivable that future viewdata systems will be programmed to play chess at a preselected level of skill. They could also play other games of almost any kind. Many games generate puzzles which players devise to tease or test each other's skill, and these too could provide a fruitful source of leisure-filling material. Viewdata could offer puzzles of the more traditional kinds as well: crossword, jigsaw, mazes, cyphers and so on. A new kind of puzzle solving is provided by programming a computer, and personal computing is becoming a hobby for the more technically minded as the cost of microcomputers falls; this also is a market that is expected to boom.

Because it offers the possibility of correspondence between its customers a viewdata system could encourage the development of common-interest groups, or 'invisible clubs', for example a group interacting and competing in the setting and solving of chess problems. These location-independent associations would establish informal links across and between communities, and perhaps eventually between nations provided that the cost of telecommunications continues to fall. Such groupings could produce significant and beneficial social changes.

In these, and other, ways computers seem likely to help us to fill our excess leisure at whatever level of activity we choose, from the hypnotic spin of a fruit machine's dials to the mind-stretching battles of n-dimensional chess.

5.7 Coda

This sketch of what computers may do to offset the

increased leisure that they will have helped to create is not
meant to suggest that there is any quick technical fix for what
will undoubtedly be a stubborn social problem. At most it is
intended to show that there is a little to be said on the other
side, and to suggest that with ingenuity and a genuine concern
to help to solve the problems of people as well as those of
production something can be done in mitigation. The problems
of education and of leisure existed before we began to use computers, and it would be foolish to allow our use of these machines to distract our attention from more fundamental questions
that remain to be answered. These are not human and social
only; they involve economic and political considerations: for
example, those related to the allocation of resources to the
construction and operation of leisure facilities at the expense
of other socially desirable projects; and the perennial conflicts between conservation, housing, recreation and farming in
our use of the countryside.

5.8 Bibliography

The influences of automation on leisure, and as a cause of
alienation, are discussed in
Problems of an Industrial Society, by William A.Faunce. McGraw
    Hill, 1968.
Leisure is the subject of a full-length book:
Leisure, Penalty or Prize?, by Ralph Glasser. Macmillan, 1970
and is considered in
Social Issues in Computing, by C.C.Gotlieb and A.Borodin,
    Academic Press, 1973.
The changes which technology may bring to every aspect of our
lives, education included, are painted in primary colours in
Future Shock, by Alvin Toffler. Pan Books, 1971.
Computer-assisted instruction and education for leisure are de-
scribed by cheerfully optimistic technocrats in
The Computerized Society, by James Martin and Adrian R.D.Norman.

Penguin Books, 1973.

EXAMPLES 5

(5.1) 'Leisure, like money, can only be evaluated in terms of the value of the ends it is used for.' Say whether, and why, you agree or disagree with this statement.

(5.1) Not all of non-working time is leisure. List its other components, and comment on how you expect them to be affected by the increasing use of computers.

(5.3) What do you consider should be the function of technical education in a period of rapid technological change?

(5.4) Choose a subject which you consider to be well suited to computer-assisted instruction, and one that is not. Give reasons for your choices.

(5.5) Chesterton once wrote 'Art is the signature of man'. What does that imply for the role of computers in the arts?

6 · The domesticated computer

6.1 Introduction

The very high costs of setting up a production line for microelectronic circuits, and of programming a microcomputer application, imply that one of the more profitable outlets for microcomputers will be the mass domestic market. This is an area of use that will affect each one of us directly and intimately, but also insidiously for we will not necessarily know that we are, in fact, using computers. In much the same way few of us are aware of just how many electric motors we use for everyday purposes in our homes. It seems likely that separate microcomputers will be used for each domestic function performed, because it will be cheaper to do this, and more flexible, than to program a single microcomputer for multipurpose use.

Vigorous attempts will undoubtedly be made to achieve sales volumes large enough to justify the faith displayed, and to reward the investments made, by those *entrepreneurs* who have already installed massive production units. Some will succeed simply as microelectronic hardware manufacturers, but there will be wider opportunities for employment and profit in supplying systems and appliances which derive their competitive edge from using microcomputer control to enhance their performance. Many such products will be advertised as 'intelligent', but this will be a misnomer. They will not display curiosity, adaptability to unforeseen circumstances, or that selection of their own goals and objectives which we associate with human intelligence. Nevertheless, they will be much more effective and helpful instruments than their non-computer competitors and predecessors; and they might reasonably be distinguished by the English adjective 'competent', or the American one 'smart'.

It is easy enough to suggest possible uses for microcomputers in the home, but impossible to predict which of them will be taken up. Certainly, there will be powerful and sustained attempts at selling, but these goods will be luxuries rather than necessities. Hence, the rate and depth of penetration of this market will depend critically on our general economic circumstances, and on what other goods will appear to compete for our favour in this hazardous arena. For these reasons this chapter is unavoidably a collection of recipes rather than a treatise on dietetics, and it claims to do no more than show how wide a range of choices is open.

6.2 Some household systems

6.2.1 *Heating*

The increasing demand for central heating and our growing concern for energy saving are opening up a fertile field for the domestic use of microcomputers. They could provide a much more flexible and adjustable control of heating and hot-water systems than the usual time switch-cum-thermostat. Thus, with sensors in every room, and individual remote controls of radiators, it would be possible to program separate heating cycles for the various parts of a house, corresponding to their different patterns of use, and designed to conserve energy overall. The room sensors could be much more subtle than simple thermometers, for as well as responding to temperature they could measure the balance between radiant and convected heat, and the humidity and movement of the air. The control computer could be programmed to produce a combined evaluation of these components in terms of human comfort, and to take account also of the special requirements of indoor plants, antique furniture, paintings and so on. In short, a computer-controlled system could provide whatever refinement ingenuity might suggest, or affluence afford.

Energy saving will require the system to respond to the rates of heating and cooling, and to changes in external conditions - both seasonal and hour to hour - in order that, for example, heat pumps and solar panels could be combined with a conventional boiler to achieve the best result. The computer would also monitor the consumption of electrical energy to ensure that lights and appliances are not accidentally left on all night. Programmed control for the domestic hot-water supply could match the input of heat to the predicted principal requirements for baths, cooking and laundry, and so minimize heat losses incurred by having too much hot water available too soon. The best results would be obtained only by careful programming, which would involve more forethought and planning than is usual in domestic life, and perhaps more than many people would find acceptable.

6.2.2 *Safety*

The microcomputer installed to control the heating system, or more probably an independent one, could carry out simple safety checks: for instance

(a) of a fire alarm based on sensors responding to high temperature or to smoke;

(b) of leakage-current meters revealing actual or incipient electrical faults;

(c) of gas leak sensors for detecting escapes from cookers, boilers and other appliances;

(d) of a frost thermometer controlling emergency heating elements to protect water pipes and greenhouse crops;

(e) of water flow indicators able to detect burst pipes, leaking radiators or running taps.

6.2.3 *Security*

The domestic possessions of an affluent society are tempting targets, and need protection against theft. A domestic

microcomputer could readily be programmed to monitor various
kinds of intruder alarm, ranging from simple switches on doors
and windows, or pressure pads in paths and corridors, to sonar
and infrared beams guarding the open spaces around the house.
It could also control and time the recording of all calls to
the telephone, or at the front door. Individually programmable
electrically operated bolts could provide greater security than
traditional mechanical locks, for the codes that open them can
be quite complex and yet may easily and frequently be changed
by the householder. Similar locks could be used for the doors
and the ignition of the family car which, with other moveable
possessions, could be plugged in to the house alarm system.
The possibilities are endless; the problem will be to decide
what is worthwhile, or what insurers may require.

6.3 Domestic appliances

The writers of science fiction, and of the more technocratic prophecies, foresee the use of computer control for a
wide variety of domestic appliances. And, just as the availability of cheap, reliable electric motors has transformed
these appliances, so the advent of cheap portable and reliable
microcomputers will undoubtedly bring some at least of the predictions out of the realm of fantasy and nearer to realization.

Cookers are already equipped with simple electrical controls for time and temperature, but an electronic system could
be programmed to select for itself an appropriate cooking
regime when provided with data to indicate the chosen recipe,
and the time when the dish is to be eaten. It may be that our
simple cookers will be replaced by cooking machines equipped
with automatic hoppers to supply the common ingredients in
metered quantities direct to the cooking vessels. The freezer
and refrigerator would be incorporated in this machine, which
would initiate thawing at the appropriate time and use micro-
wave and pressure cooking as well as more traditional methods.

Washing machines, also, have crude time and temperature controls, but could be programmed to select the correct cycle of washing, rinsing and drying for specified weights and mixes of fabrics. For both cookers and washers the consumptions of energy and water could be minimized in the interests of economy and of conservation. In such ways as these, the housekeeper would no longer have to worry about the details of methods or the constraints of optimization, but would only have to decide what result was to be achieved.

Computer control would enable knitting machines to execute stitches of all known varieties, and to combine selected standard pattern elements specified by the user, after automatically adapting them to the measurements of the intended wearer. Sewing machines, also, could offer indefinitely wide choices of stitches and stitching arrangements; and they might be used with a cutting machine which could shape a length of the chosen fabric to a selected standard pattern, after adapting it to the wearer's current dimensions. Once again, it is difficult to set limits to what inventiveness could produce, or to decide what salesmanship might persuade us to purchase.

6.4 Miscellaneous services

Obviously a domestic computer could assist household budgeting by providing a range of calculation services: for instance,
(a) keeping current accounts of income and expenditure;
(b) keeping other financial records for tax and insurance purposes;
(c) providing reminders of payments due;
(d) monitoring public utility and other regular bills by comparing them with corresponding periods in previous years in order to check for errors and to detect significant changes in consumption;
(e) operating a 'budgetary control system' designed to ensure

that known future commitments can be met;

(f)   performing calculations for the financing of major items
of expenditure such as house purchase, car renewal, holidays, and so on.

Ordinary people using these services would rapidly be made aware
of the need for an accurate and disciplined input of data, but
many of them might find this uncongenial, and hard to learn.

As well as performing the office of Household Treasurer,
the computer could act as Domestic Secretary by keeping records
of correspondence and of engagements and other commitments.
Each member of the household would have his own pocket quartz-
crystal clock and calendar-cum-diary, which would be plugged
into the household system from time to time to exchange data,
to coordinate timetables, and to initiate reminders about car
servicing, licence renewals, appointments, anniversaries, and
so on. The previous chapter touched on the use of microcomputers to fill our leisure hours, and with the expanded telecommunication services postulated below they could provide
comprehensive information, education and entertainment services. In these various ways, therefore, domesticated computers could perform for everyone the offices of steward, secretary, tutor and court jester previously available only to
the very rich.

6.5 Telecommunications

6.5.1 *Household communications*

It is not obvious why there should be so large a ratio
between the amounts spent by a typical family on motoring and
on telecommunications, even allowing for the differences in the
methods used to sell them. Few British households are equipped
with more than one simple telephone (and it is idle most of the
day) but the use of digital microelectronics - microcomputers
especially - is opening up tempting commercial opportunities
for a very substantial enlargement of facilities. Viewdata

systems are the obvious example; and their appeal will be
greatly increased when they are permitted to offer a message
service (electronic mail) as well as information.

We may also see a developing use of automatic 'tran-
sponders'. These are devices which can *transmit* or *respond* to
telecommunication signals, and when fitted to a domestic telephone a transponder would enable the householder, away from
home, to dial his own number and follow it with a coded signal
which would cause the transponder to

(a) repeat any messages received and recorded;

(b) interrogate the domestic computers to check and report on
     the safety and security status of all systems;

(c) command these computers to adjust the heating, start the
     cooking, or carry out some other remote-control function.

Reports and messages from the transponder would be sent either
as synthetic speech, or as data signals to be displayed on a
portable terminal rather like a pocket calculator.

The same transponder could be used by public utilities to
read their meters, since metering would probably be carried out
by measuring instruments connected to the household computers.
When we add the use of telecommunications to provide selective
services of television news, teaching and entertainment, which
could be transmitted by night and recorded for reproduction at
times to suit the individual, it is clear that there is great
scope for developments that could significantly alter the pattern of domestic life over the coming decades.

6.5.2 *Shopping from home*

There will be strong pressure to use viewdata systems for
advertising. This might initially take the form of classified
advertisements in a kind of electronic Yellow Pages Directory;
it would develop naturally into the electronic equivalent of a
mail-order catalogue - all illustrations and unrepeatable offers. As well as goods, the advertisements would cover travel,

holidays, sports and entertainments. The attractions of viewdata for advertisers will be that orders can be placed at once
through the customer's terminal, and perhaps also paid for at
once by direct credit transfers between accounts. This method
might well extend to retail sales of all kinds, and the establishment of 'telemarkets' delivering to their customers' doors
would mean that no one need leave home for routine shopping.
Eventually, perhaps, one of the household computers could itself compile the regular shopping lists, interrogate suppliers
and place the orders to minimize the total cost.

Shopping, however, has social as well as economic functions. It provides opportunities for the members of a community to mix, for friends to meet, for exercise, and for
pleasant occupation; many people would miss these benign side-
effects. The decline of shopping, by leading to the closure
of shops, would have unfortunate consequences for the appearance and activity of town centres. It is important, therefore,
to ensure that the logic and economics of the computer suppliers and their system designers do not, incidentally, muti-
late our towns.

6.5.3 *Working at home*

Some attention has been given to the problems and possibilities of working from home by using a computer terminal installed and paid for by the employer. This 'telecommuting'
would obviously save a great deal of time, temper and energy
now wasted in travelling to and from work; removing the need
to travel would also help the physically handicapped. Noise,
pollution and congestion in city centres would all be reduced.
Married women could work part-time from home when their children were young.

In principle, many office jobs could operate in this way,
since they depend on the processing and exchange of information
rather than on being physically present in any particular work

66

place. Indeed, it is surprising that we have been so slow to exploit the decentralizing potential of traditional telephone and telex services. But here, also, the emptying of central office blocks would have drastic consequences for urban life and planning, and for the economics of the transport industries. On the other hand, telecommuting could provide very valuable job opportunities in rural areas.

An American study showed that not everyone would welcome the opportunity of working at home. Domestic accommodation and arrangements have not been planned to cope with full-time active occupation by all members of the family; thus only the larger houses and flats have space in which the worker could operate without domestic interruption or disturbance. Again, as with shopping, many men and women enjoy interacting with others outside their family, both at work and on their crowded journies. The loss of these opportunities for wider contacts would reinforce the trends which already exist towards the fragmentation of the community into isolated individuals, and that would be a social change to be regretted. Isolation would also cut off professional men and women from the easy everyday exchange of ideas with their peers and colleagues.

6.6 Some social consequences

Clearly, computer-assisted automation is potentially as pervasive and powerful an influence in the home as it is at work, and might end by relieving men and women of much routine activity. We could then reach the condition which Aristotle imagined would be necessary for the abolition of slavery, namely 'that each inanimate instrument could do its own work at the word of command, or by intelligent anticipation'. The combination of microcomputer control with electric motor driving power could indeed emancipate us from the slavery of domestic routine. In doing so it would, however, add to the 'burden' of leisure, and some of us may decide to continue to exercise our

muscles and relax our minds as we busy ourselves with undemand-
ing chores. We might so choose either on the moral grounds that
work is good for our souls, or because most people would rather
be busy than bored, or for the pragmatic reason that many of us
do not find it possible to stay on the peak of our creative form
all the time, and immersing ourselves in 'necessary' routine
work avoids or postpones the need to face that disturbing fact.

Of course, it by no means follows that everything that is
technically feasible will be done. Although strong commercial
interests will seek to exploit the burgeoning capacity of the
microelectronics industry, much will depend on the general economic situation, on the attitudes of society to what some may
see as a 'frivolous' use of scarce resources, and on the common
sense and sales resistance of individual customers.

6.7 Bibliography

An imaginative scenario of life in a computerized household is included in

Living with the Computer, edited by Basil de Ferranti. Oxford
University Press, 1971.

The Computerized Society, by James Martin and Adrian R.D.Norman.
Penguin Books, 1973.

Computers and the Year 2000, edited by Lord Avebury, Ron
Coverson, John Humphries and Brian Meek. N.C.C. Publications, 1972.

Each of these accounts antedates the microcomputer, and they do
not assume that computers will be cheap enough to allow the use
of separate microcomputers for different domestic systems and
appliances. The effects that electronic development in telecommunications may have in reinforcing the withdrawal of individual men and women from community life are disconcertingly
presented in

The Private Future, by Martin Pawley. Pan Books, 1975.

EXAMPLES 6

(6.1)   What behavioural characteristics would a computer system
        need to display to be correctly judged 'intelligent'?

(6.2)   What advantages could be gained by applying microcomputer
        control to domestic heating and hot-water systems? What
        disadvantages might be incurred?

(6.3)   'Today's domestic cookers will evolve into automated
        cooking machines.'
        Say why your agree, or disagree, with this statement.

(6.4)   Criticize the judgement that
        'The "office in the home" will not come: people prefer
        to work in a social environment.'

(6.5)   Mark Twain wrote
        'Civilization is a limitless multiplication of unnecess-
        ary necessaries.'
        How far does his criticism apply to the prospective uses
        of computers in the home?

7 · Privacy and the protection of data

7.1 Introduction

Of all the social changes that may be produced by our use
of computers none has received more attention than 'the invasion of privacy' which it is feared may accompany the processing of personal information. This subject came to life in
1966 in America when it was proposed to establish a National
Data Centre which would collect and collate information then
being held piecemeal in the separate computer files of the
Agencies and Bureaux of the U.S. Government. The objectives
were unexceptionable: to improve accuracy, efficiency and economy, not to increase surveillance. However, as an American
judge, Justice Louis D.Brandeis, observed in 1928: 'Experience
should teach us to be most on our guard to protect liberty when
the Government's purposes are beneficent... The greatest dangers to liberty lurk in insidious encroachment by men of zeal,
well-meaning but without understanding.'

After lengthy hearings before a Congressional Committee
the proposal was shelved, but public discussion of the risks to
the privacy of individuals continued, and this subject now has
a longer bibliography, of lower quality, than any other connected with computing. Another result has been that special legislation has been enacted in several countries, and is under con-
sideration in others.

7.2 Privacy defined

One dictionary defines privacy as 'Being withdrawn from
society or public interest; avoidance of publicity'. In these
ordinary senses most of the actions that disturb our privacy
have nothing to do with computers: for instance,

(a) having our personal affairs reported in the press;

(b) being televised as a member of the crowd at a football match;

(c) being quizzed for a public opinion poll or market survey;

(d) being photographed without our knowledge or consent by a remote or concealed camera;

(e) being overheard by a long-range microphone or an electronic 'bug';

(f) having advertising literature and other unsolicited mail thrust into our letter box;

(g) being questioned about a journey by traffic-survey officials.

In general, there has been no specific legal right to privacy, although respect for each others' privacy is widely regarded as a mark of civilized behaviour. In the context of computing, privacy refers to a person's right to control the provision and use of information about himself. Six principles have been enunciated which reflect that right; namely that an individual must be

(i) made aware of the existence of any file that contains information about him;

(ii) able to discover what information is held, how it is being used, by whom, and for what purpose;

(iii) able to correct errors in this information;

(iv) able to challenge its relevance to the stated purpose;

(v) able to prevent information obtained for one purpose being used for another without his express consent;

(vi) assured that whoever holds and processes his data takes reasonable precautions to prevent its misuse.

7.3 Personal data files

Personal data include

(a) descriptive information: for example, identifying characteristics, measurements and so on;

(b) records of activities, such as financial transactions,
     medical treatment, education and so on;

(c) inferential data: for instance, records of attendance at
     meetings, membership of societies, and so on.

To be classified as personal these data must clearly be associated with a named individual, or be capable of being traced to
him.

Records of personal data have, of course, been kept for
centuries before the use of computers. They can be divided
into two principal classes depending on whether the data in
them is to be used to affect someone directly as an individual, or whether it is to be used for research or as a general
guide in the formulation of policy. Thus:

(a) *Records that affect individuals directly*

    (i) Administrative records fill a wide variety of
governmental and commercial files. Birth, marriage and death
records are examples of data that are regarded as public property. Records of our interactions with the tax, health and
social service authorities are more private, although many officials need to see and use them in the ordinary course of
their work. Court records relating to bankcruptcy also concern
very personal matters, but are open to general inspection in
the public interest. Most of the administrative records kept by
commercial organizations relate to money matters: payroll, bank
accounts, hire-purchase ledgers, insurance policies, bills for
goods and services, and so on. The data in them is held in
confidence unless and until the business is required to produce
it as legal evidence.

    (ii) Intelligence records are designed to provide per-
sonal information to help public authorities (for instance,
police and national security services) and others (for example,
providers of commercial credit) who, in circumstances relevant
to their function, need to be able to assess, predict or

influence the behaviour of a named individual. Records of this type are rarely published, except in a court of law, and often their existence is not known to those who feature in them.

(b) *Records that do not affect individuals directly*

  (i) Statistical records include, for example, population censuses or surveys. To reduce errors and improve comparability, statistical data are often recorded in some standardized format, and usually the identity of a subject is detached from his or her data when these are being processed. Again, data for several subjects who share some common feature may be grouped or 'aggregated', and this also helps to conceal the identities of those concerned. Statistical data are commonly considered to be anonymous, and thus to present no risk to privacy. However, statistics are collected to provide a factual basis for the formulation of government policies, and by their highlighting of 'abnormal' groups there is a danger that some sections of the population – teenagers, say – may become 'statistical stereotypes', difficult cases requiring special treatment, and in this way be disadvantaged as a result of losing a kind of collective privacy.

  (ii) Research records include, for example, medical records. From the point of view of medical science there would be merit in being able to follow the progress of individuals, and to link together the records of a family or of those in a district, in order to investigate hereditary or environmental factors in a disease. This kind of requirement can be met by statistical files in which personal identifiers are replaced by arbitrary codes, and which have a separate confidential index that allows a particular item to be traced for legitimate research purposes. This is satisfactory only when it is done with the understanding consent of those whose data is to be read.

Of these four classes of record, intelligence records are potentially the most troublesome for they are collected in order to be able to initiate action which the affected individuals would have preferred to avoid. Combining items from records kept for other purposes is a well-established way of creating an intelligence 'dossier'. It is important, therefore, to observe principle (v) of §7.2 above; namely to make certain that personal data are not casually or irresponsibly passed to intelligence files from other kinds of record. In particular, data provided for statistical purposes ought not to be transferred to administrative files of either kind.

7.4 The users of personal data

7.4.1 *Public authorities*

In 1978, British Government departments maintained some 257 computer files which contained personal data. These were by no means equal in size or importance; some contained as few as 250 entries, and the largest - census records - contained over 74 millions. Personal records are also maintained by the National Health Service, Police Forces, Security Services, Education Services, Public Utilities and by Local Authorities. The list is a formidable one, and could suggest to the nervous that Big Brother may indeed arrive by 1984.

However, in a free and democratic society few of us worry much about the possibility of oppression, or of close surveillance, by our government. Many accept that a government needs a great deal of information about its citizens in order to administer with equity the complex web of legislation that directs and constrains its dealings with them. Some of us also believe that, if anything, governments are short of the information they need to frame economic and social policies which are effective, and relevant to contemporary problems and current needs. Perhaps we face the *Catch 22* situation which characterizes the early stages of all systematic studies, namely that

without information we cannot hope to achieve understanding,
but

without understanding we cannot determine what information
we need.

Fortunately we do not have to solve our problems at a stroke,
and we can hope to progress by the cyclic sequences of conjec-
tures, refutations and refinements which have been typical of
advance in the sciences.

7.4.2 *Private businesses*

A business needs to use its computers to hold personnel
records about its staff, and personal information about its suppliers and its customers. Many customers use hire-purchase, or
some other form of credit, and 'credit reference agencies' exist
to advise on their credit worthiness. Some of these agencies
will hold their records in computer files, and between them they
hold personal data on many millions of people. Indeed, the
world's largest private databank is operated by an American
credit reference agency which, in 1976, held records on 50
million people. These records are potentially troublesome for
they contain rather sensitive personal information, and their
inaccuracies have occasionally resulted in someone losing in
financial reputation, or meeting unjustified difficulties in obtaining credit. The other financial bodies that maintain personal data records include banks, insurance companies and building societies.

Those who seek to sell goods through the post also keep
records that help them to aim their 'mail shots' more accu-
rately. These records may be exchanged with other companies,
or sold to them, and their data are sometimes combined with information from published documents - such as an electoral register - to add up to what amounts to a 'dossier' on an individual.
The industry claims that the items of information on its files
are trivial and harmless; this may well be true, but their

combination may be a more potent brew.

7.5 Computers and personal data

There is no need to state in detail why computers are
being used to hold and process personal data; the benefits are
well known. Their use does, however, introduce the following
significant changes.

(a) The user organization's capacities for storing, recalling
and processing data are each greatly enlarged, thereby
removing economic and practical limitations on its appe-
tite for information.

(b) Access to data within an organization, and between organizations, is made very much easier and quicker by the use
of data communications and remote terminals; moreover,
being less obvious, it may escape control.

(c) Those responsible for keeping the records are technical
specialists who are not themselves interested in the use
of the data, and whose contacts with its providers and
users are indirect; and they tend to be more concerned
with efficiency and technique than with any social implications of what they do.

These changes help to explain the current clamour for some form
of public control.

The only complete control is to limit the input of data,
for what does not go in cannot be got out. We may, therefore,
reasonably ask that anyone who proposes to set up a new computer system to handle personal data should be required to make
a formal public declaration of

(i)   the purposes the system is intended to serve;

(ii)   how long it would be necessary for it to operate to serve
those purposes;

(iii) the irreducible minimum of personal data needed to serve
those purposes;

(iv)   the categories and numbers of persons about whom data

76

would be held;

(v)   the sources from which data would be drawn;

(vi)   the periods of time for which it would be necessary to
        hold each item of data;

(vii) which items of data could be held in ways that avoid
        linking them with identified or traceable individuals.

The intent is clear: personal data systems should be permitted
only when the purpose served is socially acceptable and necessary, and they should hold no more data for no longer period
than can be thoroughly justified in relation to their declared
purpose.

It is debatable whether personal data held in a computer
system are more, or less, secure than those stored in manilla
folders in conventional filing cabinets. A higher level of
expert knowledge is required to extract and understand computer
data than to abstract and read a paper record. However, given
that expertise, and it is not uncommon, it may be possible for
an intruder to break into a computer file by linking a clan-
destine terminal into the computer's data communication system.
It is at this point that the concepts of privacy and security
tend to merge, and this has confused many discussions of these
different matters. Security refers to the *means* employed to
protect personal data, in order to achieve the desired *end* of
preventing a loss of privacy. Computer security is considered
in its own context in the next chapter.

7.6 Some principles

Six principles were set out in §7.2 which derived from a
definition of privacy. Clearly these would apply to personal
data systems of all kinds. Six further principles have emerged
from the general discussion of privacy in computer systems.

(a)   Access to stored information should be limited to those
        authorized to have it, and then only permitted for the
        purposes declared when the information was collected.

77

(b)   For each item of data, a period should be specified beyond which it will not be retained.

(c)   Particular care should be exercised when subjective data – for example, value judgements – are recorded in the form of codes.

(d)   No more information should be collected or recorded than is strictly necessary for the declared purpose.

(e)   When personal data are collected for administrative reasons and the opportunity is taken to seek additional data for statistical or research purposes, it should be made completely clear which information an individual is legally required to provide, and which is being invited as a voluntary response.

(f)   In statistical systems the identities of data subjects should be kept separate from the rest of their data.

The close observance of these principles, and the other six of §7.2, and of adequate security precautions would do much to answer the doubts about computers and privacy.

7.7 Data protection and the law

Since 1970, seven countries have enacted laws to guard privacy by protecting personal data in computer systems; namely, Sweden (1973), U.S.A. (1974), West Germany (1977), Canada (1977), France (1978), Norway (1978) and Denmark (1978). Austria, Belgium and Luxembourg have presented bills to their legislatures.

In Britain, the government accepts that legislation is needed to make sure that computer systems holding personal information 'are operated with appropriate safeguards for privacy', and it proposes to achieve this by ensuring that personal data are protected, rather than by establishing any general right to privacy – a much more controversial matter. In December 1978 the British Government received a lengthy report which recommended the establishment of a Data Protection Authority that would register all uses of computers to process personal data, make rules to control the different kinds of uses of such systems, investigate complaints and enforce compliance with its rules. After an interval for public discussion of the report a bill will be presented to Parliament, and it could be enacted in the early 1980s.

Telecommunication channels cross national frontiers as they traverse the world or hop to and from artificial satellites, and the signals that convey computer data are virtually indistinguishable from those of other public services. It is not really practicable to institute checks on international exchanges of data. It is, therefore, highly desirable that the various national laws which protect personal data should be closely coordinated if 'transborder data flows' are not to be impeded, and yet evasions of control are not to proliferate. There must be no advantage to be gained by establishing personal databanks in 'data havens'; that is, in countries which have weak laws about privacy, or none, or whose laws apply only to data about their own nationals. Equity also requires that the computer users, services and manufacturers of a country should not be handicapped in competition with their foreign equivalents by the greater stringency of its national data-protection legislation. However, the existence of separate laws and bills in ten countries, and the fact that each has its own legal system and principles, suggest strongly that the processes of international harmonization will be as painful and as protracted as they usually are.

7.8 Coda

The discussion of privacy tends to be emotive rather than rational; and the alarm expressed relates less to the risk of embarrassing disclosures than to a fear of Big Brother, or the possibility of unjust treatment. These dangers are not confined to computer systems, but a computer's high speed of processing,

and the large volumes of data which can be economically stored
mean that it can combine and collate information that would
remain disconnected in a manual system; and as noted in the
Lindop Report (see §7.9 below):   'items of information which
are harmless in isolation can become sensitive in combination'.
The scope for combination is being further increased by the
availability of microcomputers which with data communication
networks will allow data held in separate locations to be
brought together for analysis. A databank is a concept, not a
machine; it does not have to be physically located in one
place, and in a dispersed system all the stored data can be
regarded as existing simultaneously at every point of access
in the network.

       We fear what we do not understand, and so ordinary people
fear computers more than they fear filing cabinets, and they
see the consequences of using computers to keep personal records
as constituting a social change which is potentially so adverse
as to need control by legislation. In framing this legislation,
however, we must take care not to make it so restrictive that
we frustrate or delay the beneficial social changes that might
flow from improved information about the circumstances and
needs of the population.

7.9 Bibliography

       A full bibliography of privacy and the computer would fill
the remaining pages of this book; but much of the material is
superficial or partisan. The flavour of the public discussion
can conveniently be sampled by reading the record of a 'Workshop
on the Data Bank Society' which was held in London at the end
of 1970. It appears in
Privacy, Computers and You, edited by B.C.Rowe. National Com-
       puting Centre Ltd., 1972.
Its bibliography lists over 130 publications. An excellent
American discussion of the subject appears in the so-called

'HEWS Report':

Records, Computers and the Rights of Citizens. Report of the
Secretary's Advisory Committee on Automated Personal Data
Systems. U.S. Department of Health, Education and Welfare,
U.S. Government Printing Office, July 1973.

Its bibliography lists some 300 items.

In Britain, privacy has been the subject of four government
publications:

Report of the Committee on Privacy, Chairman Rt Hon. Kenneth
Younger. Cmnd.5012, H.M.S.O., 1972.

This, the Younger Report, is a source document that is frequently referred to; it is reviewed in two White Papers issued
by the Home Office. The first of these:

Computers and Privacy. Cmnd.6353, H.M.S.O., 1975

discussed the principles, and proposed the setting up of a Data
Protection Committee to advise the government on the form of
control and to refine the objectives. Its companion paper:

Computers: Safeguards for Privacy. Cmnd.6354, H.M.S.O., 1975

provided, *inter alia*, detailed information about personal data
systems in operation in the government. The Committee produced
its own lengthy (460 pages) report in December 1978:

Report of the Committee on Data Protection, Chairman Sir Norman
Lindop. Cmnd.7341, H.M.S.O., 1978.

This, the Lindop Report, contains a useful discussion of the
subject, and much information about techniques, applications
and legislation; and it outlines proposals for a Data Protection
Authority.

EXAMPLES 7

(7.1) List six examples of intrusions into personal privacy
which do not involve the use of computers.

(7.2) Personal data files have long been kept in printed or
written form. In what ways does the use of computers
increase the risks of their contents becoming known to

an intruder?

(7.3) Discuss the problems which the continuing development of international telecommunications is posing for the protection of personal information.

(7.4) List any items of data which you consider should not be recorded in any personal information system. Give, briefly, your reasons for advocating their exclusion.

(7.5) Give two examples each where the computer records of personal information kept by the government are of benefit

(a) to the individual,

(b) to society.

8 · Crime and war

8.1 Computers and crime

Crimes that involve computers combine two highly news-
worthy topics, and there is no need to recount what has already
received headline treatment in the popular press. We need rather to consider how, if at all, the use of computers may change
the nature and extent of criminal behaviour. Computer crimes
fall into two classes:

(a) acts which damage the computer system itself, and

(b) crimes which exploit some application of computers.

8.1.1 *Crimes against computers*

Crimes of the first class are obviously a new social
phenomenon; so far, however, they have been relatively few in
number and not very important. In some instances, disgruntled
computer staff have sabotaged or maliciously damaged their employer's computer, even to the extent of shooting at it with
revolvers. On occasions, and for ideological reasons, students
have destroyed the magnetic tapes which held their academic
records. Unsuccessful attempts have also been made by computer
staff to extort ransoms for magnetic tapes which they stole because they mistakenly believed them to contain the only copies
of essential commercial records.

These crimes against computer hardware have their software
counterparts. Software can be damaged by introducing deliberate
errors; it can be destroyed by erasure, and it can be stolen.
Some have speculated that an unscrupulous programmer might conceal a self-rewarding, or a destructive, sequence of instructions in an application program or in the software controlling
the system. This sequence would normally be by-passed, but

could be triggered into action by inserting a pre-arranged code-group into the input data. The last instructions in the sequence would cause it to be erased, thus destroying the evidence, and for this reason the technique has been dubbed a 'logic bomb'.

It is also possible to steal computer services. The staff of a computer centre may themselves use the system without payment, or sell its use to outsiders; and they may conceal their crime by entering data to mislead the accounting routines, or by altering the operational log to skip over periods of unauthorized use.

8.1.2 *Crimes against computer applications*

Many computer systems hold and process confidential information which can be stolen and misused. Personal information of a potentially damaging kind could be copied and used for blackmail. Commercial information, for example contract proposals and prices, or details of new products, could be stolen as an act of industrial espionage. Most of the reported computer crimes, however, have been concerned with financial applications, and have followed the well-trodden paths of fraud, theft and embezzlement. The new features which computers introduce are speed and inconspicuousness, for the criminal act can be confined to a brief period of illicit operation from a remote terminal, and the corresponding action inside the computer system itself is still briefer and even less apparent. The methods used have not, so far, been particularly subtle, nor in most cases have they required a high level of computer knowledge.

For instance, a pay clerk has been known to substitute his own pay number in other employees' input data about overtime; the names of imaginary employees and of dead pensioners have also been used to enrich the criminal. Bank employees have diverted deposits to the account of a non-existent customer, from which they have later drawn cash. Some computer systems round down small amounts - British banks, for instance, do not deal in halfpence - and instructions have been fraudulently inserted into an accounting program to accumulate the roundings in a fictitious account; this has been called the 'salami' technique, for the criminal helps himself to many very thin slices. Again, charges for goods and services have been inflated, and goods have been diverted by entering false delivery instructions.

Most of these subterfuges result from someone's realization that there are exploitable weaknesses in the design of a system's checking procedures. None of them is specific to computers. Computer crimes, therefore, tend to be the same old crimes adapting themselves to a new environment; but what about the criminals?

8.1.3 *Computer criminals*

The evidence suggests that computer crime is a white-collar occupation for younger men. Many of those who have been caught have been first offenders who were previously considered by their employers to be reliable, honest and intelligent. Their crimes have not involved personal violence, and they have damaged a large machine system or an impersonal organization rather than visible and vulnerable human beings. The offenders, therefore, tend not to be concerned about the moral aspects of their actions, but rather to worry about the risk of exposure and the social injury that this would cause to their families and friends. Relatively few of those who have been detected have been computer specialists, but most of them have been connected in some way with the legitimate use of the system. Computer crimes are insider jobs.

Some commentators, anxious to defend computer systems, suggest that they are in fact safer than manual ones, with proportionately fewer crimes reported (although the sums of money lost on each occasion have been much larger). However, this may not be the true picture for it seems clear that a number of cases which have been exposed by audit, or revealed by accident, have not been reported to the police or pressed to trial. A business which has suffered losses may prefer to absorb these rather than advertise the weakness of its financial controls, or destroy its customers' faith in a computer system, which moreover it would be costly and very troublesome to abandon or alter.

Despite the publicity that computer crime has attracted because of its science-fiction flavour and its intriguing hint of super-crooks, it seems likely that our use of computers has not significantly increased the amount of crime. Nevertheless, the public will continue to enjoy the myth of the criminal genius, for it serves the dual purpose of making life seem more exciting - and at someone else's expense - and of confirming the suspicions that ordinary men and women have about computers. The principal social change might be an increase in the number of first offenders drawn from clerical and managerial jobs.

8.2 Police and security

8.2.1 *Introduction*

Computers may not be adding appreciably to the amount of crime that the police have to handle, but they are being used by them in the fight against it. Police work inevitably requires a delicate balance to be struck between the liberty of ordinary citizens and the close surveillance needed for the detection of crime and the arrest of suspects. The police's use of computers could disturb that balance, and cause unwelcome social changes.

Those who design and operate computer systems have a duty to make them secure. They owe this duty first to their clients, whose money or confidential information may otherwise be lost; and they owe a duty to society not to tempt its weaker members into crime. To understand what is involved we need to consider

briefly the nature of the threats, and the methods available
for defence, in computer systems. Crime also includes crime
against the state, and there are aspects of national security,
and of defence, which involve uses of computers that could
have implications for society.

8.2.2 *Police work and computers*

Our concern is not with the day-to-day management of a
police force, for that closely resembles the management of any
other organization, but with the provision of the information
- the criminal intelligence - on which successful police work
so heavily depends. Because motorways enable criminals to
travel far and fast, police information must be available
nationally and immediately. In the computerized database of a
national police force it is useful to record information about

(a) known criminals,

(b) missing and wanted persons,

(c) stolen vehicles,

(d) vehicle owners,

(e) drivers' licences.

Many other items could also be of legitimate interest to the
police, but these few will suffice to illustrate the difficulty
of reconciling the liberty of the people with the efficiency of
their police.

The recording of information about known criminals appears
to be necessary and acceptable provided 'criminal' and 'information' are each appropriately defined. Criminals are clearly
those who have been convicted of serious offences, but should
there be a limit of time after which reform may be presumed?
And what is 'serious'? Should minor offences such as obstruct-
ing the police, or petty theft, be included? Such hard information as name, date of birth, and physical appearance is beyond
reasonable objection, but what about more speculative material
such as unproved criminal activity, or suspicious associates?

The extent and use of criminal intelligence information, much of which may be less than certain, and not all of which is clearly relevant, are key questions. Lists of cars, owners and drivers are obviously of great value, but they also allow the police to trace the movements of citizens who may be mistakenly suspected of involvement in a crime, say because their car was quite innocently parked in what became the vicinity of a crime, or was borrowed or stolen in dubious circumstances. Similarly, the reasons for listing missing and wanted persons are clear enough, and should cause no anxiety provided that the police's reasons for 'wanting' someone are socially acceptable.

It will be apparent from the foregoing that the fears that have been expressed about the use of computers by the police relate to the nature of the records they keep, and the use they make of them. Computers fan these fears by increasing the efficiency of record keeping, and by removing the restrictions on the accessibility and volume of recorded material that constrain manual methods; but the prime cause of concern is rooted outside computing. Our attitude to police records essentially reflects our attitude to the police. If we believe that they can and should be trusted, then our fears will be minimal. Because this is a desirable state of affairs our concern should be to encourage the police, by external advice and lay supervision, to continue to operate with an acute sense of social responsibility. Of course, a happy acceptance of this view will come less readily to members of minority groups which the majority find odd or disturbing - anarchists or drug addicts, for example. But it would be unfair and futile to blame the police for reflecting the general attitude, and crassly stupid to curse their computers, or to deny them that help in fighting crime.

8.3 Computer system security

8.3.1 *Introduction*

The increasing use of computers in all our affairs, and the possibilities of computer crime, require security precautions to be taken if adverse social consequences are to be limited. However, because they codify and restrict the working conditions of those who use or operate computers, these precautions are themselves troublesome; they are also expensive, and we have to strike some sort of balance of disadvantage in which the level of security matches the level of risk. Broadly speaking, the precautionary measures available are of three kinds: physical, computer-based and administrative.

8.3.2 *Physical security*

A computer installation must be protected against natural hazards and human malice by keeping up-to-date copies of its working programs and data files in a separate 'disaster store' which is located at a sufficient distance to be safe from any fire or flood that may affect the computer centre. Damage by hostile human action can be reduced by exercising strict control over access to operational rooms, including the disaster store, through the use of security guards, pass cards, electronic locks, intruder alarms and the like. It is also important that 'waste' of all kinds - paper, carbons and printer ribbons, magnetic tape and so on - should be destroyed by shredding or burning to prevent the illicit recovery of the information recorded on it. In particular, because most computer crimes have been committed by trusted insiders, there must be stringent control over the removal of punched cards, magnetic tape or disks and printed output by anyone. Where the need for security is particularly high, care will be taken to detect the use of electronic bugs, and metallic screening will be used to confine the radiation of electromagnetic signals from the equipment or its communication links.

8.3.3 *System security*

The design of a computer system should incorporate security measures from the start, for it is difficult and expensive
to graft them on later, and the result is rarely satisfactory.
The aim should be to restrict, or detect, unauthorized access
to programs and data; some of the ways of doing so are listed
below.

(a) Segregate the data and program files of different users,
and note that this shuts out the advantages of using a common
database. In extreme cases it may be necessary to schedule
separate periods for processing sensitive work, and to purge
the system of all programs and data before and after each such
period.

(b) Check all messages from remote terminals in order to restrict the use of the system to identified and authorized
persons, who are operating from the terminal they are permitted to use, at the prescribed times and for certain clearly
specified purposes only. The current forms of identification
are a password, or a coded magnetic card; more secure forms
may in the future depend on biometric data such as voiceprints
or signature analyses.

(c) Log the patterns of operation by individual users, and
from individual terminals, and of access to individual records
and programs. Any significant change in use, such as an increased volume of messages to and from a particular terminal
or file, or a change in its times of use, or in the types of
transactions would be detected and reported to the security
controller.

(d) Encrypt all messages to and from terminals, and possibly
all data in files, and change the encryption key frequently
enough to limit the risk of disclosure by a corrupt or compro-
mised employee.

For these, and other, measures to be effective it must be

impossible for a terminal user to seize control of the operating-system software. This can be achieved by having a separate piece of software which can be accessed only from one privileged terminal, and whose task it is to monitor and control the execution of all security measures. Alternatively, an independent supervisory computer can be used.

8.3.4 *Administrative methods*

The most important administrative contribution to security is to ensure that only reliable staff are employed, for dishonest persons with inside knowledge can frustrate any security precaution. The organization of work should respect the well-established principle of the 'separation of functions'; for instance, those who make outpayments should not also authorize them. Regular financial audits, and random security inspections, are proven administrative methods for ensuring conformity with the rules and preventing the onset of complacency. It is also salutory, and may be humbling, to commission independent experts to attempt to penetrate the security of the system in order to reveal its flaws.

8.3.5 *Coda*

Security cannot be achieved without cost and effort. Its costs include the salaries of security staff, purchase costs for alarms, locks and other equipment, design costs and some reduction in operating efficiency and flexibility. There are also adverse effects on the attitudes and morale of the staff, for they will be chafed by identification procedures and access controls, and disturbed by the general atmosphere of suspicion. Finally, given time and sufficient motive a determined computer expert can penetrate the security of even the most complex system. So far, however, high professional expertise has not been applied to computer crimes - or, at any rate, not to those unsuccessful ones which have been detected.

8.4 Computers and war

8.4.1 *Introduction*

The day-to-day control of an army, navy or air force is
very much like the administration of any other large organization, and the use of computers for these housekeeping purposes
raises no social problem beyond those raised by similar uses in
business and industry. Indeed, to the extent that they make
defence forces more efficient, computers free resources for
application to more direct and obvious benefits to society.
The potentially disturbing changes are those that may result
from the direct military applications of computers to weapons
and to intelligence work.

8.4.2 *Automated weapon systems*

Computers can be programmed to act as extremely effective
automatic controllers, and without their aid it would not be
feasible to use many current weapon systems. Consider, for
example, a rocket designed to destroy enemy missiles. A warning that missiles have been launched, and a plot of their
flight trajectories, will be given and continuously updated
by long-range radars. These use computers to process their
reflected signals in order to disentangle those generated by
an enemy attack from the confusing background of radio noise,
interference and friendly signals. Other computers will combine data from a number of different radars with that from
satellites and other sources to maximize the information presented to the defence commander. It is for him to decide to
initiate a counter attack and to designate its targets, but
then ground computers will calculate the flight paths for the
intercepting missiles, aim them and determine the correct
times to fire. Continuous control will be maintained in flight
by on-board computers in each missile, and they will also determine when to explode its warhead.

These and other straightforward applications of computers

to weapon-system automation may not appear to have much bearing on social change. However, wars and the needs of defence have always produced very rapid accelerations in the application of science, for the task is accepted as urgent and important, and massive resources are made available. It has been the insatiable demands of space exploration and defence - and the two are connected - which have fuelled the development of microelectronics and, as a side-effect, initiated the social changes that are of so much concern today. The complex offensive and defensive weapon systems which use computers have undoubtedly changed the relations and tensions between the major powers, and thus altered the risks of war. The military use of computers has also changed the threat to ordinary people, but the outcome is not clear for it is possible to argue either

(a)   that the intercontinental missiles they make possible would hit the civilian population population harder than the simpler weapons of earlier wars, or

(b)   that computer guidance allows these missiles to be directed more precisely at military targets.

8.4.3 *Military intelligence*

A simple and effective way of obtaining information about the capabilities and intentions of a potential enemy is to accumulate and analyse every scrap of data that comes to hand. Some of this will derive from openly published material, some from reconnaissance and some from the interception of signals emanating from the enemy's territory and from his operations overseas. Clearly the great capacity of computer systems for storing and correlating information - the very features that give rise to fears about privacy - are of immense help in intelligence work. It is not possible to say whether a general improvement in military intelligence would advance or retard the cause of peace; circumstances vary and there can be no final conclusion. We can be certain, however, that the advent

of computers has transformed the situation, and will continue
to do so.

8.4.4 *War games and strategic analysis*

British officer cadets were once trained in the arts of
war by TEWTS (tactical exercises without troops): more realistic simulations of battle situations can now be provided by
computers driving suitable displays. These war games can be
increased in size and complexity, and let us hope in realism,
in order to provide models of full-scale wars in which a nation
may be involved with a range of potential enemies, and a variety of allies. To the extent that these simulations can be
made adequate for the purposes of strategic analysis they
should help to ensure that the military advice given to governments will be soundly based. We can welcome any changes in
this direction, for they are likely to discourage mere adven-
turism. It is, perhaps, fortunate that this stabilizing influence is most likely to operate in the nations which are
most advanced in their use of computers, since they are also
those whose weapons could cause the most human misery.

8.5 Bibliography

There are a number of accounts of computer crime, but few
analyses. Two useful books are
Computer Crime, by G.McKnight. Michael Joseph, 1974.
Crime by Computer, by D.B.Parker. Charles Scribner's Sons,
    1976.
Computer security tends to be treated as a collection of
recipes, but
Security for Computer Systems, by M.A.L.Farr, B.Chadwick and
    K.K.Wong. N.C.C. Ltd, 1972
presents a systematic account, and has a bibliography. The
military uses of computers are not widely discussed, for obvious reasons, but articles are published from time to time

in the computing and technical press.

EXAMPLES 8

(8.1)   Write notes on two computer crimes which you have seen
        reported in the press, with particular reference to the
        use of computer expertise by the criminal.

(8.2)   Some computer experts believe that they should be organ-
        ized as a profession, with a code of ethics. Discuss
        the relevance of this to the prevention of computer
        crime.

(8.3)   'The use of computers by the police brings the police-
        state ever nearer.' Give your reasons for agreeing, or
        disagreeing, with this statement, and indicate any re-
        straints which you believe should be placed on the use
        of computers in police work.

(8.4)   Write notes on the principal methods of making computer
        systems more secure. Whose responsibility is it to bear
        the costs involved?

(8.5)   In what ways might computers be used to reduce the risks
        of war?

9 · Systems and society

9.1 System integrity

In the previous chapter we looked at the precautions
needed to discourage computer crime. It is important also to
ensure that computer systems do not become a social nuisance,
or a hazard, by being a source of errors, and in particular of
unsuspected errors or inadequacies. Errors can arise in a number of ways and afflict all stages from initial input to final
output.

(a) Input data may be incorrectly scanned by automatic
readers, and human operators can make mistakes when entering
data through a keyboard. Various checks can be made to indicate the presence of an error. The simplest, but not the
cheapest, is to enter the data twice and compare the two ver-
sions; if they agree there is a high probability that no mistake has been made, if they disagree then the whole process is
repeated until they do agree. Or again, a batch of items of
numerical data may be added together on a pocket calculator
and the total entered as a tail piece to the batch, this 'sum
check' total is then compared with the result of performing
the same addition by the computer on the stored batch of data
once input is complete. Quite often input errors are gross
ones which can be exposed by a 'credibility check': for instance, no date requires a month of more than 31 days, and no
employee can work for more than 168 hours in one week. The
various processes of 'data vetting' absorb computer time, but
experience shows them to be essential, and a nice judgement
has to be made by the system designer as he weighs the de-
creased risk of error against the increased cost of checking.

(b) Data may be lost or corrupted in transmission over the

cable or radio channel that connects a computer centre to a
remote terminal. This can happen when electrical noise and
interference are picked up, when disconnections or other
faults occur, or when maintenance engineers are working on the
equipment. Many different techniques are available for pre-
serving the 'integrity' of data communications; they range from
methods of handling the electrical signals themselves to clever
ways of encoding the data so that any errors introduced in
transmission can be detected, or even corrected, automatically
provided that they do not occur too frequently or too close
together.

(c) Data can also be lost or corrupted in the processes of
storage and retrieval inside the computer system itself. Magnetic tapes and disks can be adversely affected by dust and
humidity, and high-speed electronic stores can be upset by
power failures and electrical disturbances. The remedies are
twofold. First, remove the cause by using air-conditioning to
extract dust and control humidity, and by fitting regulating
circuits and electrical filters to smooth the power supplies.
Then, as in transmission systems, special codes can be used to
check and correct occasional errors.

(d) Errors in programs, more commonly known as 'software bugs',
can present considerable difficulties. They are of three main
types:

(i)   logical - where the programmer has made a mistake
        in the analysis of a process;

(ii)   syntactical - where an instruction is erroneously
        expressed in a way that breaks the rigid and formal-
        istic rules which govern most programming languages;

(iii)   transcription - where there has been a copying or
        input error.

A major commercial program contains several tens of thousands
of instructions, and some of them are 'conditional jumps' which
enable the computer to select alternative routes through the

program in order to adapt its processing to the data and the circumstances it happens to meet. Commercial programs have a particularly high proportion of jumps, hence the total number of possible routes through such a program is so very large that it is just not feasible to test every possible combination. Nor can we even be sure that some months of trouble-free use will have explored every recess in the program. It is not possible, therefore, to be completely certain that a program of realistic size is ever free from error. This doubt applies not only to the individual application programs that users prepare for their own work, but also to the large master program - the operating system - which controls the execution of all other programs processed by the system. Indeed, experience suggests that large programs reach an equilibrium state in which the acts of searching for and correcting errors themselves introduce as many new errors as they remove. The removal of errors, 'debugging', is an art which absorbs large amounts of programmers' time and, because it depends on detective flair, individuals who are equally intelligent and equally well trained can differ widely in their ability to debug.

(e) A program may be reasonably free from errors but be unsuitable because its system designer has failed to meet its user's needs either

(i)   by specifying inadequate or inappropriate procedures; or

(ii)   by failing to foresee and provide for all possible combinations of circumstances.

(f) the operators at a computer centre may mount the wrong tapes or disks, give incorrect commands from the console, or make other mistakes through lack of skill, inadequate information or carelessness. Fortunately most of these errors produce such gross results that the system 'crashes', work is halted, and the only penalties are costs and delays.

In the different ways reviewed above a computer system may generate errors, or fail to match the expectations of its users. In some circumstances these failures cause no serious or irreparable damage, or damage that is limited to an immediate user who has to pick up the pieces as best he can. When, however, the consequences of failure are more widespread it becomes desirable to double-check the system design by making a kind of 'integrity audit', and independent experts may be employed for that purpose. For example, we might expect such an audit to be a prerequisite for a computer system which is to control air traffic, or which will monitor and regulate a nuclear reactor.

9.2 A highly strung society

The economic factors that affect the mass production of goods and services have favoured

(a)   the development of specialization - the division of labour in the interests of efficiency;

(b)   the substitution of capital for labour - first mechanization, now automation, soon robotics;

(c)   large-scale operations - to spread the high fixed-costs of a capital-intensive process over the largest possible volume of products.

The first and the last of these trends are somewhat contrary, and their combination succeeds only when there can be a close integration of the activities of separate units which are not necessarily owned and controlled by a single organization. Successful integration within a company, and externally between it and its suppliers, requires a copious and rapid exchange of information. That exchange is ideally suited to computer systems, and the use of computers has greatly helped to enlarge the scale of operations, which has now achieved world-wide proportions for the larger multinational corporations.

The result is efficiency, but the price is interdependence,

for the tightly spun web of relationships is sensitive to disturbances in any of its parts. In particular, it is susceptible to difficulties in the information system itself. This not only heavily underlines the importance of integrity, reliability and security in that system, it also places a greatly increased bargaining power in the hands of those who work with its computers and communications. The more active trade unions, being well aware of this development, have taken pains to recruit computer staff, for these provide them with an instrument for applying instantly painful pressure to a recalcitrant employer. Moreover, as these unions expand and diversify, their computer members become available to take 'industrial action' on behalf of other, and quite unrelated, sections of the membership as well as in their own cause. The effects of their action are quickly felt, and because they are relatively few in number it would be possible to support them in it indefinitely by a modest levy on the whole membership.

Trade unions normally act against an employer in pursuit of the immediate microeconomic objectives of their members, but there are other pressure groups with less limited aims - ranging from international political factions to the merely crackpot. Because computer systems are designed and operated by small groups of men and women, these teams could be infiltrated over a period in order to gain a position from which to threaten, or to cause, a costly disruption unless or until some demand is met - in a kind of data hijack. The spreading use of computers is undoubtedly changing the information infrastructure in ways which increase the vulnerability of an individual organization, and which also considerably enlarge the extent to which its paralysis will spread to dependent activities and functions in other parts of our tightly strung society. We may need to consider how far we dare go before 'closely integrated' becomes dangerously 'highly strung'.

9.3 The systems concept

Every age exists in a climate of opinion that largely determines which problems it worries about, and sets the criteria by which solutions are judged to be satisfactory. In our age the climate has been predominantly scientific, and most of those engaged in the study of men, women and society have sought academic respectability by adopting the methods of science. Two of the more fashionable scientific paradigms are 'systems' and 'cybernetics', and because computers are themselves designed and operated as cybernetic systems it is only to be expected that in using them we treat society as some kind of super-system comprising political, cultural, economic and other sub-systems. We may adopt this approach entirely pragmatically with no attempt to decide, or even to ask, whether it is a true mirror of reality, and use it only because it offers a powerful and fruitful line of attack. There is, however, a risk that when we have to deal with those large areas of human activity that have not been consciously planned we will try to force them also into the mould of rational systems. Many of our institutions and relationships seem to have evolved as mere congeries - as casual associations in time and space - in which no one has bothered to reconcile conflicting elements. Even our more rational organizations exhibit substantial elements of contingency.

If human societies act as systems, they cannot be closed ones for they are deeply involved in major interchanges with their environment. One property of open systems is 'equifinality' - the ability to reach the same end by alternative routes - and the stability shown by our complex societies suggests that they do in fact share this characteristic. We are today aware of the environment and our impact on it to a degree that our fathers would have found incomprehensible, or even faint-hearted. We take pride in our sensitive, humane and responsible response to the range of problems conveniently

covered by the emotive term 'pollution'; although a cynic might
see our much professed concern for the environment as a convenient rationalization of the old policy of seeking to extend
a society's sphere of influence in order to insulate it from
unsought and unwelcome changes. In the planning of industry,
transport, recreation and housing we seek to design our 'natural' environment and our activities as a harmonious whole, and
the drive to consider society from the systems point of view
draws strength from our wish to bring our affairs under closer
control, so that we may avoid Emerson's reproach that 'things
are in the saddle and ride mankind'.

The systems approach makes heavy use of mathematical and
econometric modelling to reveal the effects of assumed interactions, and to predict the consequences of alternative policies. Some pessimists have foreseen that as these techniques
of 'social engineering' are extended we shall evolve towards
a cybernetic state with totally planned and tightly knit economic, cultural, political and social systems. However, those
who happen to dislike the prospect of becoming ciphermen in
cyberland can draw comfort from the facts that some pundits
doubt its possibility, and others deny its value. Even if we
knew enough to embark on the planning, prediction and exact
analysis of social policy, its application could be effective
only in a highly ordered and well-structured society. Such a
society would also tend to be stagnant and resistant to change,
and because survival depends on making effective responses to
totally unexpected challenges it might not endure.

In our daily lives each of us plays many different, and
not necessarily consistent, parts. This multiplication of
roles provides a connective tissue of cross-ties between components of society that might otherwise be separate entities,
as for instance between parents who happen to have children
attending the same school, but who differ in politics, religion, education and economic class. These cross-links make

102

it tiresomely difficult to split a society cleanly into dis-
tinct sub-systems for the purposes of analysis or control, but
they also provide stability and durability. How otherwise
could the ship of state have escaped wreck when it has been
navigated for so long on the basis of untested economic hypotheses and untestable political slogans. The necessity of survival has encouraged the evolution of policy-proof social systems in which we can change some parts and some relationships
without igniting a train of consequences that destroys the
whole. However, our existing social systems have been selected
by their resistance to the sporadic and limited changes of the
past, and it does not follow that they will be able to survive
the very rapid changes now being imposed on them by the unprecedented pace of technological development - not least in
the technologies of communication and computing.

9.4 Coda

Systems analysis has been very successful in the design of
machine complexes for defence, air-traffic control, automated
production and their like. It is tempting, therefore, to apply
it also to the less determinate, less quantitative, problems of
society; but here we must proceed with care and with hope, recalling always Lord Shaftesbury's observation that a system
provides 'the most ingenious way of becoming foolish'. We face
complex interactions that exist and have important consequences,
and which events force us to influence whether we understand
them or not. As a practical matter we have found that we can
isolate pieces of most problems, analyse them as sub-systems of
some whole, and arrive at helpful conclusions. Our use of computers is allowing us to calculate the behaviour of systems of
very much greater complexity than has hitherto been practicable,
and we may hope that the systems we are now able to construct
will more closely reflect the stupefying complexity of the real
world, and so help us to understand the springs of our own

behaviour.

But, as we construct our systems we do well to recall that our brains are probably the product of an evolutionary selection of those fittest to survive. Survival seems likely to have depended on the relevance of our ancestors' responses to appetites and threats, and on their adaptability to change. None of these attributes requires an accurate or complete understanding of the environment, but only a sufficient congruence with the run of events in that local segment and epoch which our progenitors happen to have experienced. This line of thought gives no assurance, therefore, that the world is necessarily intelligible to us - not even that small, anthropocentric, but vital, corner of it we call 'society'.

9.5 Bibliography

Computer system integrity is well discussed at a detailed level in

Integrity and Recovery in Computer Systems, by T.K.Gibbons.
    N.C.C. Publications Ltd, 1976.
The general concept of systems is a topic that was helped to rise to popularity by the publication of
General System Theory, by Ludwig von Bertalanffy. Goerge
    Braziller, 1968.
A good introductory review appears in the Open University's reader,
Systems Behaviour, edited by John Beishon and Geoff Peters.
    The Open University Press, 1972
and
Tools for Thought, by C.H.Waddington. Paladin, 1977
provides an idiosyncratic, popular and readable guide.

EXAMPLES 9

(9.1)   Using as your example a radio channel linking a remote
        terminal to a central computer, distinguish between

'integrity', 'reliability' and 'security' as applied to computer systems.

(9.2)   Devise credibility checks for the following items of input data:

   (a)   a schoolchild's age,
   (b)   the time of day,
   (c)   a patient's weight (NB check units),
   (d)   the consumption of sugar by a hotel,
   (e)   the quarterly gas meter reading for a domestic consumer.

   List three items for which no credibility check is possible.

(9.3)   Write brief notes on the ways in which a computer program may fail its user.

(9.4)   What are the significant facts about computers which a trade union leader needs to know?

(9.5)   Define the concept 'system', and comment on its applicability to

   (a)   economics,
   (b)   sociology.

10 · Computers and democracy

10.1 Introduction

It may not be immediately apparent why our use of computers should be expected to have any effect on the processes
of democracy. Few people worry about the use of slide rules
or pocket calculators; indeed, concern is more often expressed
about the lack of 'numeracy' among the electorate. The new
factor that computers introduce is the fact that their combination with communications has given men and women the most
powerful information systems that they have ever had. These
systems are not equally available to every section of the population, and their use could shift the locus of effective political power away from ordinary citizens. Again, some technically minded enthusiasts have proposed to speed up the electoral process by the use of electronic techniques, but without
considering the wider effects of modernizing this ancient piece
of political machinery.

'Democracy' is a word with many meanings. Until this
century it tended to be a term of abuse - meaning mob rule -
but it is now more often appropriated as a mark of approval,
or at least of self-justification. In this chapter 'democracy'
is used in the restricted sense of 'representative democracy',
and more specifically to denote the current form and style of
parliamentary government in the United Kingdom.

10.2 The will of the people
10.2.1 *Opinion polls*

Representative democracy implies government with the
consent of the governed, and that in turn implies that there
are effective exchanges of information and opinions between a

government and its subjects. The built-in way for the citizens of a democracy to impress their views on their government is to refuse to re-elect it, but this method has the defect of being sporadic, infrequent, and often less rewarding than you hoped. To bridge the gap between elections a number of organizations have set themselves up in the business of assessing the views of the public by interviewing samples of the population. The use of computers is not essential, but they are commonly employed to accelerate the process of analysis, and it is not considered to be a disadvantage that they also lend an air of scientific authority to the results.

The accuracy and reliability of the results of an opinion poll depend on many factors, for instance on the precise wording of the questions asked, on the respondents attitudes to the poll itself and to the interviewers, on how 'truly representative' the sample was, and on how stable or volatile are the views expressed. Great accuracy is not to be expected. It has also been suggested that opinion polling could introduce some side-effects with undesirable political consequences, especially when a poll is conducted immediately before an election. Thus we could have

(a) *Feed-forward effects* which might disturb the result of an impending election. Three kinds of effect have been distinguished:

    (i) *band-waggoning* which causes some undecided voters to join what the polls are predicting will be the winning side;

    (ii) *apathy reinforcement* which causes the more lazy electors not to bother to vote because the polls have predicted that the party they favour will win by a handsome margin;

    (iii) *back-pedalling* which causes the timid to refrain from voting for a party which has been predicted to win easily, in order to prevent it from having the power of too massive a majority.

(b) *A feedback effect*, when polling is combined with the techniques of market research to put together a shopping basket
of policies designed for maximum electoral appeal. At
first, they may seem to represent a highly democratic response to the expressed wishes of the people. However,
all reservations about polling accuracy apart, reflection
suggests that this approach would degenerate into a slick
sales exercise which would produce oven-ready packages of
popular nostrums, rather than a coherent and responsible
program of legislation. Were that to happen, the electors
would slip from their status as the ultimate political
masters to become the pliant consumers of government goods
and services, whose prejudices and preferences could be
manipulated by the irrational 'hidden persuaders' used so
effectively in retail selling.

10.2.2 *Electronic referendums*

The referendum is now established in the United Kingdom
as a way of determining the will of the people. Some electronic enthusiasts have seen this as a development which offers
a splendid opportunity to install an automated voting system
with remote terminals in polling stations connected to a central computer that totals the vote, and is able to declare the
result without delay. They claim that in this way the entire
population could vote on every major matter of policy, and
that this would revive the true spirit of democracy. We need
not pause to consider the contemporary relevance of the ancient
Greek system, nor how many of the inhabitants of Athens were
excluded from voting, for this is a proposal which confounds
the mechanics of voting with the essence of democracy. That
essence is not to be found in the detailed arrangements for
determining the will of the majority, but in the elected majority's respect for the rights of minorities.

A widespread use of electronic referendums would alter the basis of electoral choice from the selection of party programs to the determination of individual issues, with all the problems of *ad hoc* coalitions that this could bring. Moreover, many of today's political questions are complex and highly technical, and would have to be butchered into a deceptive simplicity for the purpose of a referendum. Few men and women have the capacity to analyse such questions, and fewer still the inclination to devote the time and mental effort required to reach informed and well-reasoned conclusions. If electronic referendums were to become the rule it seems more than likely that the formidable apparatus of the mass-persuasion industry would be deployed by interested factions, and the popular vote might well be swayed by the most recent, most plausible, demagogue to appear on television. This change from representative democracy to a kind of push-button populism would be a sad decline from rational and responsible choice in our political affairs. Once the novelty had worn off, it would probably also bore the population to tears.

10.3 Computer modelling and political choice

Many of the choices which face governments today are too complex for unaided analysis, and computer models (see chap.3) are being increasingly used to provide rational bases for decisions. In this situation the politicians retain their delegated authority to act, but they dare not do so until the alternatives have been thoroughly examined and their side-effects explored. Commonly the models used to guide decisions are designed by experts in the subject area, and are inherently beyond the comprehension of lay men and women. This fact raises some significant political points. The lay elector, or minister, is in the position of a ship's master entering a difficult harbour; it would be rash of him to ignore the (expert) pilot's advice but the responsibility nevertheless remains wholly with

him; if the ship runs aground the master will be blamed for
acting on unsound advice.

(a) How then, can a lay man reassure himself that the model
being used is appropriate and correct, sufficiently realistic,
supplied with adequate data and capable of providing stable
results? One way is to employ a second, independent, expert
to check the recommendations of the first.

(b) How can a minister challenge a decision which is recommended on the basis of a rational analysis by those acknowl-
edged to be expert in the field?

(c) If electors cannot challenge such decisions is this not
likely to reinforce their sense of exclusion from the political process? And, might not that lead to the taking of direct
action, for example, by public demonstrations, as a more
satisfying and effective way of influencing public policy?

(d) Is there a risk that effective political power might pass
into the hands of expert bureaucracies?

Skilful ministers know the merits of employing several experts
and exploiting their disagreements in order to reach the decisions which they wish to take on purely political grounds.
We need also to remember Lady Lovelace's comment on Charles
Babbage's invention; she wrote that a computer 'can do whatever we know how to order it to perform'. Computer models are
limited by the knowledge of those who design them; they are
the stalking horses of experts, and carry no more authority
than the men who are manipulating them.

10.4 Computers and corporativism

Representative democracy rests on the assumption that
electors and their representatives will work together in
reaching political decision, and this implies

(a) the free availability of information;

(b) the ability to draw sound conclusions from it;

(c) the right to have these conclusions heeded.

As more and more information is stored entirely inside computer systems, and is exchanged automatically between them, so it becomes inaccessible to ordinary men and women. Ironically, also, the measures which may be used to protect the privacy of personal information (chap.7) may well further reduce our access to information. These two unplanned results of using computers could strengthen the hands of those who would prefer to limit access to the data used in the formation and application of public policy. In this matter, however, the technology is neutral, for viewdata systems (chap.2) may make information more readily available to anyone who cares to pay for service.

Even if ordinary people were to obtain access to adequate supplies of information under some more open style of government, the potential volume is so great that they would not be able to handle it without the use of computers. Databanks, models and the necessary expertise are expensive items which only the larger organizations can afford to use, and ordinary citizens and their members of parliament could find themselves at an increasing disadvantage when they wish to oppose schemes proposed by major businesses or public authorities. The result could be to shift political power away from the individual elector and towards large corporate bodies. Some political commentators claim to have detected such a trend towards corporativism in the tendency of British governments to formulate economic policy in consultation between ministers, the Trades Union Congress, the Confederation of British Industry and similar large bodies. The results are then presented ready-made for formal approval by parliament.

10.5 Coda

Our eager and enlarging use of computers, and the unprecedented power of the information-handling systems they provide, must surely affect the processes of politics. It seems most unlikely that anyone is deliberately planning or engineering the shifts in political power that could result; nor is it likely that computers will be the sole cause of whatever changes occur. No iron law requires events to develop in ways that we dislike. We can, if we choose to do so, direct our future progress along paths that preserve rather than threaten our freedom, but only if we remain alert, and willing to act. Democratic government is commonly regarded as the best protection for the liberty of the subject, but apathy is its enemy, for as John Philpot Curran said 'The condition upon which God hath given liberty to man is eternal vigilance.'

10.6 Bibliography

The development of information technology and its implications are compactly surveyed in

The Changing Information Environment, by John McHale. Elek, 1976.

The U.S. Government has been active in its use of computers, and a useful study of its applications appears in

Information Technology in a Democracy, edited by Alan F.Westin. Harvard University Press, 1971.

The Open University's reader:

Man-Made Futures, edited by Nigel Cross, David Elliott and Robin Roy. Hutchinson, 1974

includes a major section on policy and participation in a democracy. The influence of experts is probed in

The Politics of Expertise, by Guy Benveniste. Croom Helm, 1973.

Democratic choice and computers was a principal theme of a European Conference whose proceedings are reported in

Human Choice and Computers, edited by E.Mumford and H.Sackman. North Holland, 1975.

Hannes Alfvén wrote, under a *nom de plume*, a brief history of the future which contains many witty and perceptive comments on life in 'The Complete Freedom Democracy', dominated by computers; see

The Great Computer, by Olof Johannesson.   Gollancz, 1968.

EXAMPLES 10

(10.1)   What are the objections to using the techniques of
market research to compile a list of policies with the
maximum electoral appeal?

(10.2)   List the factors which may reduce the value of an
opinion poll as a guide to public opinion.

(10.3)   Say why you would, or would not, support the introduction of an electronic voting system to facilitate
the holding of national referendums.

(10.4)   In what ways might the use of computers shift the
locus of political power?

(10.5)   'Unique solutions are the negation of politics.   They
remove choices from the sphere of human discussion and
judgement.'   Discuss this with reference to the use of
computer models as aids in the formation of policy.

11 · The way ahead

11.1 Side-effects and society

Previous chapters have outlined a number of ways in which
our use of computers may initiate social changes, or influence
those already in progress. We who live in the 'advanced' industrial nations can expect that most aspects of our lives will
be touched, and in some measured altered, by the use of computers. Up to now, most of these changes have been generated
as side-effects, as the unintended and usually unforeseen ac-
companiments of attempts to increase efficiency or to save
costs. As the use of computers continues to grow, and to expand into new areas, it is becoming necessary to consider
whether it is prudent to allow their rapid introduction to
continue unchecked by any kind of social control.

11.2 The case for social control

Those who favour the extension of public ownership in
industry and commerce will regard the need for social control
as self-evident, as a minor special case of their general
theorem. But even those of a contrary political persuasion
accept that social controls are needed where it is evident
that irresponsible operation would present unacceptable risks
to life, limb or liberty. There is no dispute, for instance,
that the practice of medicine should be restricted to those
who are 'properly' qualified by training and experience.

Certain applications of computers could, indeed, endanger
life - the control of air traffic and of a nuclear reactor
have already been mentioned. The mishandling of personal information held in computer files could diminish our liberty.
The economic consequences of computer-assisted automation and

robotics could threaten our livelihood; and the unchecked expansion of microcomputers into our domestic lives and leisure
will undoubtedly affect our 'quality of life'. Some, at least,
of these consequences might become troublesome enough to justify the imposition of a form of social control.

11.3 Methods of social control

The social control of computing could take various forms
with different degrees of formality and rigour.

(a) The least formal arrangement would be for the suppliers
and users of computers to volunteer to limit the rates of provision and introduction in order to allow time for social adjustment. However, it would be unrealistic to expect so altru-
istic a degree of self-control in so highly competitive a
market; nor would foreign suppliers conform of their own free
choice. It is much more likely that the rate of introduction
will be restrained by the organized resistance of those whose
work is affected. There are numerous examples of workers op-
posing the introduction of some new technology which they
feared would make them, and their skill, redundant. Often they
have forced the would-be users (their employers) to delay the
putting of their plans into effect until safeguards, transfers
to other work, and compensatory awards had been negotiated.
It is too facile to castigate these workers as reactionary
Luddites, for experience has taught them that technological
improvements have rarely, if ever, been made with the specific
objective of advancing the conditions or increasing the rewards
of the labour force.

(b) The establishment of a 'professional body' is a well-known
method of reinforcing the self-control of the experts practising
in a defined field. Its members have to meet high standards of
education, training and experience, and to accept the restraints
imposed by its written codes of professional ethics and practice. Those who offend are required to appear before a

disciplinary tribunal of their peers which has the power to rebuke or to warn them, or even to suspend or to cancel their membership. Professional bodies owe their effectiveness as social controls to these sanctions, which can either

(i)   deprive an individual of the public esteem, social status, and mutual support of his fellows which go with membership, and the confidence which it gives to his clients; or

(ii) prevent him from operating altogether when membership is a legal requirement for public practice, as in medicine.

Computing has its professional bodies - The British Computer Society, for instance - but these are young organizations which are not yet accepted by the public as the prime sources of authority in their field; membership of them is not a pre-requisite of practice; employers of computer staff do not in-sist upon it, or reward it; and many eminently competent prac-titioners choose to remain outside. In these circumstances professionalism remains a relatively weak form of social con-trol in computing.

(c)   Governments are themselves very large users of computers, and major employers of computer staff; it follows that the codes of conduct and practice which they themselves observe provide signal examples to other users. They also carry out and support research and development in computing technology and techniques, and they exert a considerable influence on the scope and scale of the teaching of computer science. In all these ways a government influences all who operate in its territory, and cannot escape from bearing the heavy burden of ensuring that its own actions help to develop a socially re-sponsible attitude among other computer users.

(d)   When all else fails it may become necessary to enact specific legislation to control the use of computers. This could take the form of requiring that all who design computer systems for certain sensitive applications shall be members of a recognized professional body, in order to ensure that its codes of ethics and practice are observed. Or the users of computers may be controlled directly by a public body appointed for the purpose - as is the case for the protection of personal data.

Laws are an effective way of punishing bad conduct, but cannot make anyone good. It is also difficult to frame a satisfactory law to regulate an activity, such as computing, whose potential is largely unknown and untapped, and whose techniques are developing extremely rapidly. Almost certainly any law will be too rigid, and will act in an arbitrary way to constrain or prevent future developments of undoubted social value. Or it will be by-passed by unforeseen advances in technology. These considerations argue for having no more legal control than is absolutely essential to protect the public, and for that minimum to be expressed in terms of broad principles rather than as a mass of detailed regulations.

(e) For the sake of completeness we should note the extreme form of legal control, namely, total prohibition. The world existed without computers, indeed many parts of it still do so, and it would not be impossible to abandon their use altogether. Even so, and attractive as such a course may seem to those who favour returning to a simple style of living, it is not one that is at all likely to be adopted. Computer systems are now so pervasive in industry, commerce and government, their provision and operation involve so much money and provide so many jobs, and the problems and costs of reverting to manual methods are so tremendous, that the chance of any democratic government winning agreement to abolish the use of computers can be wholly discounted. And no non-democratic government is likely to dispense with so powerful an instrument of social control.

11.4 Choosing our future

Given that our use of computers will continue to develop, and recognizing that the forms of social control considered above are purely negative, we are left with two alternatives.

(a) We could adopt a neutral, *laissez faire*, stance in which the development of computing is allowed to continue unchecked, as individual users happen to decide.

(b) We could attempt to steer the course of development in directions that we expect to be socially and economically beneficial.

These alternatives have rather obvious political overtones, and can be expected to appeal differently to those who favour greater or lesser degrees of involvement by the state.

It is worth noting that the more active second course implies that we possess enough data and understanding to be able to foresee our needs, and to evaluate the consequences and side-effects of whatever actions we may wish to take to direct the future course of events. Few would be bold enough to claim that this is so in computing. It does not follow, however, that we should decide to do nothing, for it is important that the 'social consequences' of computing should be the subject of public debate. To be fruitful this discussion must be based on more information than is generally available to the public at present. Crude stereotypes, wild extrapolations and an excessive sense of insecurity characterize much of the current discussion of computers by ordinary men and women. Most people dislike and resent the use of computers in applications that affect them directly, and little attempt is made to dispel the ignorance on which these unpleasant emotions feed. It is, therefore, important and urgent to 'educate' the public, for avoidable fear is a social and personal evil which we should seek to remedy. From this process of education, and from the informed public debate which could follow, we can hope to learn a great deal about the nature and the implications of

the social changes which our growing use of computers is helping to bring about.

11.5 Coda

No book which attempts to deal with the complex interaction of society and technology can hope to provide answers
to the many difficult questions that arise. Certainly, when
the technology is as pervasive and as powerful as that of the
computing-communications synergy the best that can be achieved
is to expose some problems. It is, nevertheless, important to
do this, first in order to draw the attention of computing
specialists to the wider issues raised by the practice of
their fascinating craft. It is, also, highly desirable that
those who are not specialists should be made aware of the
changes and challenges - and the opportunities - which may
arise. It is urgently necessary to provide them with facts to
relieve the fears induced by the widespread, but largely ill-
informed, speculation which is current. Computers are not the
only, nor are they necessarily the most troublesome, of the
new technologies that will affect our daily lives. However,
the economic, social and political decisions which our use of
them will require us to take are too important to be taken in
ignorance, nor can they safely be left to experts - of whatever
kind.

Index

Accounts, household   63

Accuracy   26

Acts, data protection   78

Administrative records   72

Administrative security   91

Alarm, intruder   62

Alienation   41,49

Apathy reinforcement   107

Aristotle, on slavery   67

Art, computer   54

Art, computer-assisted   54

Assessment, of technology   6

Audit, integrity   99

Authority, Data Protection   78

Automation   40

Automation, office   36

Automation, small-scale   41

Automation, weapon system   92

Back-pedalling   107

Band-waggoning   107

Black-box model   29

Brandeis, Louis D.   70

British Computer Society   116

Bugs, software   97

Check, credibility   96

Check, sum   96

Chess-playing programs   55

Code of ethics   115

Common database   13

Common-interest groups   56

Computer art   54

Computer-assisted art   54

Computer-assisted instructions
     52

Computer-assisted music   55

Computer, characteristics of   2

Computer criminals   85

Computer games   55

Computer model   29

Computer models and political
     choice   109

Computer processes   3

Computers and personal data   76

Computer specialists   42

Computing and privacy   70

Conditional jumps   97

Consultation   43

Cooker control   62

Cooking machines   62

Copernicus   31

Corporativism   110

Costs, social   7

Credibility check   96

Credit reference agencies   75

Crimes against computers   83

Crimes against computer
    applications 84
Criminal intelligence 87
Criminals, computer 85
Curran, John Philpot 112
Cutting machine 63

Databank 13
Database, common 13
Data havens 79
Data hijack 100
Data, not given 23
Data, numerical 24
Data, personal 76
Data Protection Acts 78
Data Protection Authority 78
Data protection, need for
    international agreement 79
Data, statistical 73
Data vetting 96
Debugging 98
Democracy 106
Democracy, industrial 43
Diary services 64
Disaster store 89
Dispersed systems 41
Domestic appliance control 62
Domestic computers 59
Dossiers 74
Dow Jones index 27

Economic model 29
Education 47
Education, technical 48

Electrical fault detector 61
Electronic locks 39,62
Electronic referendums 108
Electronic voting system 108
Employment and computers 37
Encryption 90
Energy saving 60
Errors, data 96
Errors, program, logical 97
Errors, program, syntactical
    97
Errors, program, transcription
    97
Ethics, professional 115
Experts in government 109

Facts, qualitative 25
Facts, quantitative 25
Files, personal data 75
Fire alarm 61
Frost protection 61

Galileo 31
Games, computer 55
Games, war 94
Gas leak detector 61
GIGO 24
Gross national product (GNP)
    26
Gross national product, growth
    of 26

Heating system control 60
Highly strung society 100

Home, computers in 59
Home, shopping from 65
Home, working from 66
Household accounts 63

Impact analysis, social 7
Index, Dow Jones 27
Industrial action 100
Industrial democracy 43
Industrialization 40
Information, availability of
 12
Information-poor 20
Information-rich 20
Information, sources of 13
Instruction, computer
 assisted 52
Integrity audit 99
Integrity, systems 96
Intelligence, criminal 87
Intelligence, military 93
Intelligence records 72
'Intelligent' devices 59
Interdependence 99
Intruder alarm 62
Invasion of privacy 70

Jumps, conditional 97

Kelvin, Lord 25
Knitting machine 63

Learning, programmed 52
Legislation and computing 116

Leisure 47
Leisure, use of 49
Lindop Report 80
Locks, electronic 39,62
Logical errors 97
Logic bomb 84
Lovelace, Lady 110
Luddites 37,115

Mathematical model 28
Market research and policy
 formation 108
Microcomputer, effects of 3,38
Microcomputer, economics of 39
Microcomputer, mass markets
 for 39,60
Microcomputer, programming
 cost 39
Microcomputers in service
 industries 39
Military intelligence 93
Model 28
Model, black-box 29
Model, computer 29
Model, economic 29
Model, mathematical 28
Modelling 8,102
Modelling, advantages of 29
Modelling, disadvantages of 30
Models and political choice
 109
Music, computer-assisted 55
Numerical data 24

Office automation 36
Office work 12
Opinion polls 107
Opinion polls, value of 107
Opinion polls, side-effects
    107

Participation 43
Personal data 76
Personal data and computers 76
Personal data files 75
Personal data, users of 75
Physical security 89
Police computers 86
Police records 87
Policy formation and market
    research 108
Political choice and computer
    models 109
Polls, opinion 107
Populism, push-button 109
Postal selling 75
Practice, code of 115
Precision 26
Prediction 5
Pressure groups 100
Prestel 14
Principles, privacy 71,77
Privacy 70
Privacy and computing 70
Privacy, invasion of 70
Privacy principles 71,77
Productivity 34
Productivity and computers 34

Productivity and employment 35
Productivity and leisure 47
Professional ethics 115
Professionalism 115
Program 2
Programmed learning 52
Programming of microcomputers
    39
Prohibition of computing 117
Public education, need for
    118
Public declaration for per-
    sonal data systems 76

Qualitative facts 25
Quantitative facts 25

Records, administrative 72
Records, intelligence 72
Records, police 87
Records, research 73
Records, statistical 73
Re-education 49
Referendums, electronic 108
Report, Lindop 80
Research records 73
Retraining 48
Robots 40

Sabbatical years 49
Safety systems 65
Salami technique 85
Security 77,89
Security, administrative 91

Security, physical 89

Security, system 90

Security, waste disposal 89

Separation of functions 91

Service industries and microcomputers 39

Sewing machine 63

Shaftesbury, Lord 103

Shopping from home 65

Side-effects 114

Signature analysis 90

Significance 26

Small-scale automation 41

Social control, case for 114

Social control, methods 115

Social costs 7

Social engineering 102

Social impact analysis 7

Social values 51

Society, highly strung 100

Software bugs 97

Staff, white-collar 37

Statistical data 73

Statistical records 73

Statistical stereotyping 73

Strategic analysis 94

Sum check 96

Syntactical errors 97

Systems 101

Systems and society 101

System integrity 96

System security 90

Systems, dispersed 41

Technology assessment 6

Telecommunications authority,
role of 16

Telecommuting 66

Telemarket 66

Telemetering 65

Trade unions and computers 100

Transborder data flows 79

Transcription errors 97

Transponder 65

Transponder, applications of
65

Typesetting 36

Values, social 51

Viewdata 14

Viewdata and instruction 53

Viewdata and leisure 56

Viewdata, policy for 15

Voiceprints 90

Voting system, electronic 108

War and computers 92

War games 94

Washing machines 63

Waste and security 89

Water leak detector 61

Weapon system automation 92

White-collar staff 37

Working from home 66

Working week 44

Work sharing 44

125